the series on school reform

Patricia A. Wasley
University of Washington

Ann Lieberman
NCREST

Joseph P. McDonald
New York University

SERIES EDITORS

(Continued)

the series on school reform, *continued*

Beating the Odds

High Schools as Communities of Commitment

JACQUELINE ANCESS

Foreword by Linda Darling-Hammond

Teachers College, Columbia University
New York and London

Published by Teachers College Press, 1234 Amsterdam Avenue, New York, NY 10027

Library of Congress Cataloging-in-Publication Data

Ancess, Jacqueline, 1943–
    Beating the odds : high schools as communities of commitment / Jacqueline Ancess.
        p. cm. – (The series on school reform)
    Includes bibliographical references and index.
    ISBN 0-8077-4356-9 (cloth : alk. paper) – ISBN 0-8077-4355-0 (pbk. : alk. paper)
    1. High schools–United States–Case studies. 2. Youth with social disabilities–Education (Secondary)–United States–Case studies. 3. School improvement pro-grams–United States–Case studies. I. Title. II. Series.
    LB1607.5 .A43   2003
    373.973–dc21   2002040925

ISBN 0-8077-4355-0 (paper)
ISBN 0-8077-4356-9 (cloth)

Printed on acid-free paper
Manufactured in the United States of America

09 08 07 06 05 04   8 7 6 5 4 3 2

For My Mother and Father.

"There's a dozen tricks to find your way—listen for the rut of the shore, call out and hear the echo off the cliffs, feel the run of current beneath you—or smell the different flavors of the coves. Me dad could name a hundred miles of coast by the taste of air."

—Annie Proulx, *The Shipping News*, p. 176

Contents

Foreword

The many shortcomings of large, factory-model high schools have been documented repeatedly for at least 50 years, and many studies have consistently found that, all else equal, students achieve at higher levels and feel more supported in smaller, communal school settings. Compared to schools of several thousand students in which students rotate at a dizzying speed from one teacher to the next and teachers see 150 or more students daily, small schools are particularly successful for students who often struggle educationally: recent immigrants, those with a first language other than English, and those whose families struggle economically and socially in harsh environments. Noted school reformer Deborah Meier has observed that in a large school, about 200 students have a small school experience because they are academically successful, connected to clubs and extracurricular activities, and known by the faculty. Other students are barely known. As one New York City student, a budding sociologist, noted when he was interviewed after dropping out of a large high school:

> I had passing grades when I decided to drop out. Nobody tried to stop me. Nobody cared. None of the counselors paid any attention to me. The only time I ever saw the principal was when I got sent to him, which I never stayed around for. The individual classes were too big for students to learn; students should have longer exposure to individual teachers. If students could have the same subject-teachers throughout their high school careers, this would allow teachers to get to know students better. No high school should have more than 400 students max, and all on one floor. Who needs seven floors in a school?

As the successes of some extraordinary small schools have become more widely known, reformers have started new small schools in cities from Boston to Los Angeles. The middle of the country is equally engaged: Chicago has major redesign work underway, and Indianapolis recently announced that it will restructure all of its large high schools into small learning communities. The Bill and Melinda Gates Foundation has provided millions of dollars in grants across the country to support the launching of new small schools that offer democratic communities focused on authentic performance for students in low-income communities. It would appear that change is in the wind.

Yet the hard work is just beginning. In the many eras of reform that have swept across American schools, good ideas that rest on sound research often falter in implementation, that giant "slip between the cup and the lip." While smaller, more personalized learning communities have shown better outcomes for many students, not all small schools have succeeded, and many urged to "adopt a reform" have not understood the key elements that have led to the accomplishments of others.

In this book, Jacqueline Ancess has given us a great gift. She has written an impassioned and well-documented study of how educators have created high schools that succeed in offering an education that supports both competence and community—one that cares for students successfully while it enables them to achieve intellectually. These schools, Ancess argues, function as "communities of commitment," and she provides a vivid picture with rich detail that depicts how these communities have come to be and how they actually work.

The schools are very different from one another—a school in Long Island City that serves recent immigrants who have not yet learned to speak English, a "second chance" school in Manhattan that serves students who have not succeeded in other high schools, and a consolidated vocational–technical school in a once rural area of Delaware that serves students who would not normally engage in significant academic work. Yet these three schools also have a great deal in common. Educators in all of the schools have developed a collective perspective on performance among the faculty and students; created challenging, authentic tasks and assessments as the Maypoles around which curriculum unfolds; and discovered ways to provide students with personalized support as they tackle rigorous work. These are schools that have bridged the chasm between the child and the curriculum that Dewey described by pursuing work that is both rigorous and relevant and by setting standards that improve the quality of teaching as well as levels of learning. By creating means for schoolwide collaboration and a common purpose, they function as communities that are committed to student learning—a rare phenomenon in an education system where most teachers must function in isolation from one another. This book provides rare insights into how these communities have been created—and how similar communities can be constructed by other committed educators—from an author who has herself been deeply involved in this work as both an educator and a researcher. This book rings true; it offers insight, and it offers hope.

Linda Darling-Hammond

Acknowledgments

For this book I am indebted to many people and many experiences. Any insight I have about teaching, learners, schools, and districts I developed by working in the New York City school system—for 23 years—as a teacher, school leader, and district administrator. There are many people I encountered along the way to this book: the students to whom I taught English and reading in the late 1960s and early 70s at Niles Junior High School in the South Bronx and who in turn taught me how to be a teacher; my first principal, Dr. Mildred Abramowitz, who told me, years before I could understand, that I had to care enough to teach my students; Anthony Alvarado, the Superintendent of District 4, who gave me the opportunity to start a school when people thought starting a school was crazy; Marsha Lipsitz, Phyllis Tashlik, Danny Kotok, and the late Gil Rodriguez, my partners in school creation; the 75 Manhattan East pioneer families who believed in a small group of teachers enough to entrust their children to us and start the school with us; brilliant, indomitable school practitioner colleagues and friends such as Ann Cook, CeCe Cunningham, Steve Godowsky, Herb Mack, Deborah Meier, and Eric Nadelstern.

This book would never have been written without:

My mother who, from childhood, encouraged my imagination, writing, and independent thinking; and my father, whose lifelong reflection and compassion created space in my universe for ideas about a better life for people.

Linda Darling-Hammond, whose idea it first was that this research could be a book, who encouraged me to study how schools succeed with disenfranchised youth, who nurtured me through the research, and who never tired of pushing my thinking; Maxine Greene, who many years ago reconnected me to my voice and has been a spiritual mother; and Ann Lieberman, on whose support I could always count.

Lunches with the intrepid and marvelous Carole Saltz.

I am most grateful to the teachers, school leaders, and students who gave me access to their classrooms, their work, and their inspiring stories and wisdom, who created and keep alive these three wonderful schools, and who demonstrate every day the great possibilities of public education.

Research on these three schools was supported in part by grants to the National Center for Restructuring Education, Schools, and Teaching (NCREST) at Teachers College, Columbia University from the National Center for Research on Vocational Education at the University of California at Berkeley, the DeWitt Wallace Reader's Digest Fund, the Spencer Foundation, and the Center for Collaborative Education. I thank my NCREST colleagues who make working full time and writing a book possible and a joy.

CHAPTER 1

Schools as Communities of Commitment

"I remember not being able to approach any of my teachers."

—a student

THE CALL FOR A DIFFERENT TYPE OF HIGH SCHOOL

"The case against factory-like schools that process masses of students," asserts Arthur Powell, "is apparently settled. Almost everyone wants schools to provide significant individual or personal attention, and to be places where students are known and cared for as unique people and learners" (1996, p. 1995). Indeed, for more than three decades before the Columbine tragedy, an impressive number of esteemed scholars have been making a compelling argument against the large comprehensive, factory-model high school. Their litany of complaints is long and runs deep, including not only an impersonal and uncaring environment, emotionally distant social relations, weak group cohesion and communication, high levels of anomie, silencing, disengagement (particularly among low achieving and racially, culturally, and linguistically different students), but also the production of low-level academic performance, intellectually superficial and unchallenging curricula, disempowering and unresponsive pedagogy, racial, and socio-economic stratification, retreat from shared responsibility, culture of coercive compliance, breakdown in human commitment, and faulty foundation for building a democratic social life (Bryk, 1994; Darling-Hammond, 1997; Darling-Hammond, Ancess, & Falk, 1995; Etzioni, 1993; Lee, Smith, &

Croninger, 1995; Oakes, 1985, 1995; Lee & Smith, 1994; Lee, Bryk, & Smith, 1993; McLaughlin, 1994; Glasser, 1992; The Institute for Education in Transformation, 1992; Fine, 1989, 1991; Apple, 1990; Bryk & Driscoll, 1988; McNeil, 1986; Sizer, 1984; Sorensen & Hallinan, 1986; Powell et al., 1985; Goodlad, 1984; Anderson, 1982; Fuller, Wood, Rapoport, & Dornbush, 1982; Chambers, 1981; Newmann, 1981; Rosenbaum, 1976; Rist, 1973; Baker & Gump, 1964).

Nor do these comprehensive high schools, as James Conant (1959) hoped when he proposed them, deliver on their promise to provide a rich array of resources, such as well-equipped science and language laboratories and diverse elective courses that increase students' educational opportunities and respond to their diverse interests. Numerous New York City, Philadelphia, and Chicago comprehensive high schools are known for their outdated libraries and ill-equipped, deteriorated, and unusable science laboratories. And elective courses that might have appealed to students' interests have been virtually eliminated in response to the proliferation of state graduation exams that have swept across the nation.

Because comprehensive, factory-model high schools turn out to be no less toxic for teachers, student alienation and teacher burnout are not infrequently locked in a vicious cycle (Lee, Bryk, & Smith, 1993). Bureaucratic rigidity undermines individual teacher knowledge, judgment, and dedication, which are at the core of teaching work and effective student learning. No less pernicious are the *bargains* in which disempowered teachers and students trade off low instructional demand for student compliance, undermining high performance standards, rigorous and supportive instruction, and students' intellectual development (Powell et al., 1985; Sedlak et al., 1986; Sizer, 1984; Boyer, 1983). Students' pursuit of their studies in order to achieve high grades (and standardized test scores) substitutes for intellectual engagement, which is driven by enthusiasm for the subject matter (Powell et al., 1985). Ironically, the current score-driven, high-stakes standards, standardized tests movement, where only scores matter, further undermines intellectual development. Instead of more powerful teaching for in-depth understanding, which high standards should imply, all-test-preparation curriculum prevails.

Since the early 1990s new high school models, striving for increased personalization and pedagogical responsiveness, have punctuated this scene in the form of small schools—including schools within schools, charter schools, and theme schools. Although recent research shows that on all indicators, all types of students do better in small-size schools (Ancess & Ort, 2001; Howley & Bickel, 2002; Lee & Loeb, 2000; Wasley et al., 2000; Raywid, 1999; Fine & Somerville, 1998), small size and personalization alone do not result in high-quality teaching and learning. However, when personalization, powerful teaching, and intellectually demanding learning come together in a school, as they do at Paul M. Hodgson Vocational–Technical High School, International High School, and the Urban Academy Laboratory High School–the three schools featured in this book–a compelling and impressive story unfolds about the achievements of conventionally marginalized students, about the daily, lived lives of students and teachers in their school, and about the idea and the possibility that public high schools can be humane, intellectually vital, caring, and personally responsive places. What makes these schools successful where others have failed? From the schools' own stories, what emerges is that they are communities of commitment. This chapter introduces the schools featured in this book, discusses the idea and characteristics of schools as communities of commitment, and outlines the book's organization.

WHAT MAKES SCHOOLS COMMUNITIES OF COMMITMENT?

The idea of schools as communities of commitment draws from and builds upon the culture of the three schools, themselves, and from existing, diverse, and rich literature on community and commitment.

Community

Community denotes a cohesive, self-governing, and interdependent social unit where the constituents share values and a common experience and have a sense of belonging, mutual concern and support, ownership, and habits of cooperation (Mitchell, 1968; Raywid, 1988; Kerr, 1996). Trusting, horizontal relationships, not formal externally imposed regulations and hierarchies, are the building blocks of communities (Lee, Bryk, & Smith, 1993; Goodlad, 1996). Networks of collaborative and collegial interactions, propelled by a common ethos, are the basis of decision-making and organizational integration and support a culture of commitment (Lee et al., 1993; Rowan, 1990). In a school that is a community, education occurs as a "form of community life" (Dewey, 1966/1916, p. 238).

As Greene points out,

> Community cannot be produced simply through rational formula-
> tion or through edict. Like freedom, it has to be achieved by persons
> offered the space in which to discover what they recognize together
> and appreciate in common; they have to find the way to make inter-
> subjective sense. (1995, p. 39)

Schools in which there is the space (i.e., time and freedom to imagine
things differently) to construct a common vision and mission, both theoretically and in practice, provide faculty and students with opportunities to develop a common set of values, norms of practice, and organizational behaviors—a particular, self-defined culture—which generates
the social and educational coherence that enables a school to *achieve*, and
re-achieve, community.

However, the *achievement* of community requires more than the
space for developing commonality; it requires communication. As
Dewey noted, "Communication is the way in which [individuals] come to
possess things in common" (1966/1916, p. 4). Communication is also the
way in which individuals construct the common bonds, solidarity, mutual concern and support, and cohesion necessary for the construction and
sustainability of a community. As Dewey asserted, "To be a recipient of a
communication is to have an enlarged and changed experience. One
shares in what another has thought and felt and in so far, meagerly or
amply, has his own attitude modified" (1966/1916, p. 5). Communication
means that individuals are in the habit of giving rise to their voice,
expressing their ideas. They are in the habit of hearing the voices of others and of examining, debating, and negotiating conflict and difference
and giving ground to create common ground. Communication as discourse, conversation, and deliberation contributes to the achievement of
community—democratic community—by acknowledging self-interest and
the interests of others, by making self-interest "alive to" the interests of
others (Kerr, 1996, p. 57), by legitimizing diversity, and by producing a
symbiosis between self-interest and community need (Goodlad, 1996).
Communication produces the glue of coherence. It is the way to ensure
the continuous tending to the enduring tension between the individual
and the community. It is the way to keeping both vital.

Because schools are nested in regulation-intoxicated local and state
bureaucracies, efforts to make a school an educational community—not

to mention a community based on commitments–can be a sobering task. Compliance with hierarchically mandated regulations is the rewarded outcome–*not* communication among colleagues and students, *not* the development of a particular culture based on a common ethos, a common vision of teaching and learning, a sense of belonging and ownership. Neither bureaucracies nor faculty work rules are organized to support community. Therefore, schools that aspire to be communities inevitably bump up against regulatory constraints as well as regulators, and can find themselves as district outliers or embroiled in varying degrees of dissonance and conflict with the bureaucratic culture in which they are enmeshed.

Examples abound. After implementing a senior project that successfully improved students' academic performance standards, raised student and staff self-expectations, changed curriculum, and expanded teachers' conventional roles, Hodgson Vocational–Technical High School developed and successfully executed a comprehensive strategy to persuade district officials to make the project a graduation requirement. For years International High School regularly fought state regulators to secure waivers for its unique and unequivocally successful approach to new English language learning, which counted time for formal English language learning differently from the state formula. The Urban Academy, despite many years of high rates of graduation, college going, and college continuance, continues to wage a wide-ranging battle with New York State to secure its waiver from Regents exams so that it can continue its homegrown, rigorous assessment system that is integral to its educational program.

Negotiation skills, determination, political astuteness and vigilance, and broad-based commitment to the ideas and beliefs at the very core of each school have been required for successful navigation of what can be a sea of treachery in order to enact the organization, relationships, and pedagogy that make a school an effective educational community, one with strong bonds and strong achievement. Each challenge to the commitments of these school turns out to be a test not only of the depth and passion of their commitments but of the strength and cohesion of the school as a community that can hold on to its commitments. Although strength of commitment and community cohesion turn out to be mutually reinforcing, these tests are time consuming, exhausting, and in the view of the schools, unnecessary.

Commitment

Commitment has been defined as a "formal obligation" without any necessary correspondence to personal interest (Corwin, 1965, p. 211). Here, commitment is what the school or district or state publicly pledge to achieve with the students in its charge, and theoretically, the personal beliefs of the staff are irrelevant. School staff are obligated to compliance by virtue of their organization's commitments. The current standards/standardized tests accountability movement subscribes to this idea of commitment. Regardless of practitioners' beliefs, experiences, and professional judgments about the effects of standardized testing on curriculum, instruction, and students' learning, they are obligated by district and state policy to teach to them. Here, where bureaucratic commitment competes with individual practitioner and school commitment, undermining conflicts simmer. The result is coercive compliance imposed by those with more power on those with less power.

Commitment in an educational context is also viewed as a social contract (Wehlage et al., 1989). In this view, students and school are conceived as "exchanging commitments": in exchange for school adults providing students with respectful relationships, concern for and help with personal problems, "meeting institutional standards of success and competence," and links to their future place in society, students reciprocate with respectful behavior toward adults and peers and engagement in schoolwork, which is thought of as necessary for their achievement (Wehlage et al., 1989, pp. 119–120). Commitment as contract aims to promote students' conformity (i.e., willing compliance) to the school's expectations and is motivated and sustained by the promise of future rewards.

More commonplace conceptions of commitment include the idea of a promise, attachments, involvement, and "a giving made with trust" (Steinmetz, 1997, p. 264). Greene asserts that commitment must be rooted in the personal, in particular in a personal ethos, in caring, and in bonding with others and ideas (personal conversation, 2001). One must absorb these ideas and others into oneself so that they become integral to one's identity, how one sees and defines oneself, so that any sacrifice or abandonment of these ideas and others becomes a betrayal of self and community and therefore unacceptable. It is this understanding of commitment—where personal and organizational commitments converge, where self-interest and community interest converge, where new and common ground is constructed–that one finds in operation at the three schools discussed in this book. It is this understanding of commitment that gives reason to schools' struggles with their regulatory agencies and importance to reciprocity, to mutual interest, attachment, commonality, and ownership. In this conception of commitment, power relations are dynamic, not fixed; students influence school and teacher decisions and the school and teachers influence students' decisions. Because personal conviction is an important component of this concept of commitment, the conformity and surrender implicit in and acceptable to other notions of commitment are inappropriate. This means that the school culture must be able to tolerate tensions evoked by differences.

The correspondence between personal and school commitments is important not only conceptually, but practically and operationally. Because Hodgson, International, and Urban Academy (UA) have a customized and personalized–even idiosyncratic–set of commitments, which extend faculty and students beyond the contractual and regulatory obligations of the system the schools inhabit, commitments can be *enforced* only voluntarily.[1] Without teachers' personal affiliation, the schools' capacity to honor their commitments would be limited. It is the correspondence of self-interest and the schools' commitments that drives teachers to *voluntarily* work beyond the contractual day and expand their role beyond the limits of content area instructor.

Teachers at Hodgson, International, and UA meet regularly with individual students and with colleagues who share their students to plan collaboratively curriculum, instruction, and student interventions. They play central roles in school administration, governance, leadership, and policy making. These opportunities for regular communication about the work and mission of the school help remind staff why they are doing what they are doing and what they need to do in order to achieve the school's commitments. These meetings create the time, the space, and the opportunity for faculty to revisit personal and communal commitments, their norms of practice, and the alignment of practice to student outcomes and their school's commitments. This works because the teachers are simultaneously fulfilling their own personal commitments at the same time they are fulfilling the school's commitments.

---

[1] A provision in the New York City teachers' contract allows schools to amend work rules, based on an affirmative vote of 75% of the faculty. This vote must be regularly updated.

Eliciting students' commitment also demands a correspondence with their school's mission (commitments)—as well as affiliative and affective bonds (again, commitments)—between students and teachers (Bidwell, 1965). Sizer points out that getting students to learn is linked to eliciting their commitment: "If one wants to get someone else to learn something . . . the first step is to figure out what that other person's motivations are and what strategy of incentives will hook that person's *commitment*" (1984, p. 164; emphasis added).

Urban Academy teacher Nancy Jachim contends that Sizer's hook is caring: "Kids want to be loved."

If schools expect students to embrace their priorities, Jachim contends, they need to embrace their students' priorities and be responsive to their developmental needs. They need, as Noddings points out, to develop "an ethic of care—a needs-response-based ethic [that demonstrates] how to care in [their] own relations with cared-fors" (1992, pp. 21-22) and that extends as well to the adults in the school community. How the school demonstrates caring in its day-to-day operation teaches students what caring means in the school as well as models of caring relations. The prominent role played by caring suggests that commitment contains both social and emotional (or affective) components. Social life is acknowledged and made visible, but so is the felt life.

Although caring is sometimes demeaned as "soft" or an obstacle to intellectual rigor, and although some schools that care for their students have shown insufficient care for students' learning, it is a mistake to couple caring and undemanding instruction and to dismiss the power of caring. Caring, as Jachim points out, is often the path to student learning and achievement. Caring adults in a caring school community can be the hook to achievement, graduation, and a future of meaningful options, particularly where students seem not to care about school or their future, lack confidence, and are alienated or marginalized educationally or socially because of prior school experiences or because of how they learn or do not learn, or because they are members of racially, ethnically, linguistically, or economically disenfranchised populations. "Caring teachers," claims Powell, "can help disengaged, passive, confused, or discouraged students become connected to school and to learning [by] making commitments to students and subjects regularly visible" (1996, p. 197).

Because students want to be cared for, the caring school community—one that constructs strong social and affective bonds between students and adults as well as develops a strong pedagogical infrastructure for intellectual challenge and achievement—uses caring to leverage students' commitment to school commitments because oftentimes educational, social, and emotional issues are inexorably intertwined. Caring interactions respond to all three. Caring is manifest when teachers use their in- and out-of-classroom relationships with students to catalyze, induce, and sustain student engagement and facilitate their responsiveness to curriculum tasks. Caring is manifest when teachers design curriculum and instruction to actively engage, interest, challenge, and support their particular students. Students' needs for support trigger both formal and informal, individual teacher and systemic interventions so that it is difficult for students to fall through the cracks. Teachers take the stance that students' defensiveness and resistance are obstacles *they*—the teachers individually and collectively—have to remove if they want students to make a commitment to school achievement and success. They have a sense of personal responsibility for the achievement and success of students and persist with optimism in their struggle to achieve it. This persistent struggle cannot be underestimated. It is waged and won over and over, through the daily routines of school life, through the organization, relationships, and pedagogy of these schools and through the willingness of their faculty to make change as needed, even though one would think this unnecessary because student enrollment at each of the schools occurs by a process of mutual choice. All too often the convergence of student and school commitment is accompanied by the development of a commitment to themselves and to a reimagined set of possibilities for their future.

CRITICAL CHARACTERISTICS OF SCHOOLS THAT ARE COMMUNITIES OF COMMITMENT

Schools that are communities of commitment share four common characteristics: (1) they are bound by a common ethos and vision, (2) they are caring and caregiving, (3) they possess the will and capacity for struggle, and (4) they strive for mutual accountability among all community members.

Common Ethos and Vision

At the core of schools that are communities of commitment is a common ethos about what constitutes a good education in our democratic society for the school's particular students and how that is achieved along with a common vision for its implementation. The ethos and vision embody particular ideas about our society and the modern world, the purpose of education and public schools in our democratic society, practitioner knowledge and experience, and pedagogical and content knowledge. The details of the operation of that ethos and vision, their enacted meaning, are always under discussion, review, and revision by faculty and students. The common ethos is the soul of the school. It drives all decisions about organization, roles and relationships, and pedagogy.

The common ethos creates a foundation for the school as a community by uniting faculty and students around a purpose and norms of practice—what we are here for and how we do things here. United, the faculty can confront and respond to conflicts generated by external regulations or demands. The common ethos constitutes the commitment, the promise of what can be expected from the school and those involved in it, and for what they agree to hold themselves responsible.

Care and Caregiving

Care and caregiving are systemic and embedded in the organization, relationships, pedagogy, and culture of the schools. The schools demonstrate the understanding that they need to be not only human scale but also humanized—responsive to the human need for voice, visibility, belonging, celebration, consolation, and meaning. They reject conventional high school organizational behaviors and norms that produce anonymity, anomie, isolation, invisibility, silence, insecurity, coercive conformity, meaningless rote activity, and intellectual deadening as painful and hurtful to human development, performance, spirit, and society. Care is given to what International High School teacher David Hirschy calls the "total student"—the student as a complex social, emotional, intellectual, and spiritual being. Care is given to the student as an adolescent.

Care is given to adults and to the conditions of adult work. The schools make themselves a protected public space where individual teachers have opportunities to make attachments to students, colleagues, and ideas and to develop and teach curriculum and courses that derive from an interior place of personal care, passion, conviction, and expertise. They make themselves places where teacher voice and authority over work conditions are valued and respected with the result that there are high levels of teacher trust, satisfaction, and investment in their practice and community. Teacher turnover is almost nonexistent and teachers do what they have to do in order to make their school work. Such conditions are propitious to commitment making.

Opportunities for communication are abundant and pervasive. They are embodied in the organization, human interactions, norms of practice and pedagogy, and multiple kinds of formal and informal, scheduled and unscheduled meetings among various school community members, irrespective of role or position. The schools' organizational behavior communicates their commitments.

Willingness and Capacity for Struggle

As Greene points out, community must be achieved. Commitment, too, must be achieved, particularly the commitment of students who have been marginalized and have adopted habits of alienation. The struggle to achieve student commitment is not the work of one or two teachers or a string of isolated teachers in a school. It is the work of the culture of the school community, of their norms of organizational operation, and of teachers acting together in community driven by the belief that together they can be more powerful than any one individual acting alone in leveraging high levels of student performance.

The willingness to struggle, which is crucial to students' achievement, depends upon the strength of the school's culture and commitments. The capacity for productive struggle depends on the collective knowledge and expertise of the school community and the leadership of individual practitioners. Alone, it is easy for a teacher to become discouraged and demoralized by students' resistance, or to feel overwhelmed by students' needs for interventions, or to become isolated in problem solving. As a community, the school can establish structures and interventions that support teachers' capacity to respond effectively to students' needs, resistance, and problems. As a community, a school can develop a reservoir of resilience that nurtures individuals engaged in struggles.

Mutual Accountability

Mutual accountability means that the members of the school community accept their responsibility to each other and to their school's ethos. In turn, the school as a community is responsive and responsible (Darling-Hammond & Snyder, 1992) to individual school community members for establishing and sustaining those organizational, pedagogical, and relational conditions that produce the performance standards and outcomes that have been promised. Teaching and learning are organized to engage teachers and students, to reflect their interests, passions, talents, needs, and concerns.

At the same time, teaching is deprivatized. Teachers make their practice public through peer observations, review of student work and teacher curriculum, collaborative planning and problem solving, and team teaching. They expect each other's practice to embody the ethos and pedagogical commitments of the school. The public nature of practice acts as a safeguard for the school's commitments.

School is organized for the interplay between the individual and community and to facilitate successful performance by teachers and students. Students have easy access to teachers who have opportunities to know them well as people and learners. Teachers and students are expected to use that access to develop the common ground of individual and school commitment so that there is a dynamic correspondence between student and school goals. Time and value are given to collective problem solving, self-assessment, and self-correction. The conditions exist for individuals to develop a sense of responsibility for their own as well as the common good.

A VOCATIONAL–TECHNICAL HIGH SCHOOL CAN BE ACADEMIC

Located on 44 sprawling acres, Paul M. Hodgson Vocational–Technical High School is one of three 9th through 12th grade vocational high schools in Delaware's New Castle County Vocational School District. The impeccable maintenance of Hodgson's 20+-year-old modern, two-story ranch-style building and generous grounds sends the message that this place matters. The school's carefully landscaped entrance leads to a large, carpeted, square-shaped mall with multileveled platforms that surround a center staircase leading to the school's second floor. During breaks and lunchtime, students lounge in the mall in clusters of three to ten. Some lean against the walls. Others sit on the steps to the staircase. Still others lounge on the multilevel platforms. They play cards, chat, flirt, sing, laugh, and flip through each other's notebooks. They are friendly and relaxed, making eye contact, smiling and greeting passing visitors.

Plaques honoring the teacher of the year and honor roll students over the years adorn the walls. Sports trophies, notices of upcoming events, and a listing of student government officers fill glass cases. Hanging from the balustrades of the second-floor balcony are welcoming signs and a banner announcing Hodgson's affiliation with the Coalition of Essential Schools.

Radiating from three sides of the mall, corridors lead to the student cafeteria and activities center, academic classrooms, offices, and many of the school's 22, well-appointed and resource-rich career program shops. These include heating/ventilation/air-conditioning, auto body, auto technology, carpentry, cosmetology, culinary arts, dental assisting, dental lab, early childhood, electrical trades, electronics, horticulture, information systems and services, medical secretarial, machine shop, maintenance technology, masonry, nurse assistant technology, plumbing, technical drafting, and visual communication (commercial arts), as well as drafting and technology courses. The machine, electrical, and carpentry labs are as large as small airplane hangers. Students have constructed a low-cost house built on consignment for the city of Wilmington, as well as dugouts for the school's baseball field and an addition to the greenhouse.

A new gymnasium complements several athletic fields used by the school's 12 sports teams: football, soccer, volleyball, wrestling, baseball, softball, cheerleading, and separate boys' and girls' basketball, spring and indoor track, and cross-country skiing. In the technologically modern library on Hodgson's second floor, some students work with a librarian to conduct computer searches for materials around the state for their projects. Others are in a classroom adjacent to the stacks, writing their research papers on the library's computers. In another room, students view a videotape.

Of the 985 students enrolled at Hodgson, 881 attend full time and are described by staff as almost all working class; 15% qualify for free or reduced lunch. Seventy percent are White and 30% are students of color, mainly African American. Fifteen percent are classified as special education. Approximately 20% of seniors are employed after school hours, many to supplement their family income. Some feel their job demands compromise their commitment to school academics.

Students from all of New Castle County apply to Hodgson in ninth grade for an exploratory year. The school has more applicants than spaces. If students want to continue, they must reapply for the tenth grade, and about 95% do. Hodgson rarely rejects a ninth grade student who reapplies for tenth grade; rejection only happens if students are absent for more than 40 days, which is rare (in 2001 the school's daily student attendance averaged 96%), or if they fail the ninth grade, which usually amounts to no more than five students. Hodgson and the district collaborate on admissions to ensure compliance with the districtwide voluntary desegregation plan and race and gender equity.

According to principal Dr. Steven Godowsky, Hodgson students range in academics from "high average to special education." Most have a C average. Students exhibit what teachers refer to as "vo-tech syndrome": they are antipathetic, ambivalent, undermotivated, and lack confidence in their capacity for academics. Or they are just turned off to school. Especially where academic achievement is defined by test scores and grades, students express the greatest frustration and ambivalence toward academics.

Parents, report the teachers, believe that their children, as one said, "are only this intelligent. They are only vo-tech kids. They can't do [academics]."

"[They] feel," says Godowsky, "'It's voc. I don't have to worry about academics.'"

Some teachers believe that students' attitudes are a response to previous school failure caused by prior school unresponsiveness and mismatch of prior teaching strategies and students' ways of learning. One commented:

> Some of them probably have come from schools where
> they've struggled. When [students] get hooked on shop, they
> start being more willing to do the academics. . . . Part of it is
> they enjoy the hands-on of the vocational area, whatever
> they've decided. They've found that if they exert enough
> effort they can start achieving and do well here. They find
> that they can go further than maybe if they were struggling
> in a traditional program.

Other faculty suggest that conventional measures of achievement on which students perform poorly, such as standardized tests, undermine their confidence. "During test practice, they frequently comment, 'We're just going to fill in the bubbles,'" remarked the English chair.

Table 1.1. 2001 Student Outcomes across New Castle County Vocational–Technical School District

	Hodgson	Delcastle	Howard
Attendance	95.6%	93.5%	93.6%
Graduation Rate	94.8%	96.7%	95.7%
Dropout Rate	0.8%	0.4%	0.5%
Continued Education	**70.7%**	**52.3%**	**56.9%**
Full Time	**48.8%**	**37.8%**	**35.2%**
Part Time	**21.9%**	**14.5%**	**21.7%**
Employed Full Time	41.5%	45.6%	43.2%
Employed Part Time	29.3%	32.8%	27.0%
Unemployed and Not In School	**3.2%**	**10.0%**	**13.5%**
Suspension Rate	0.06%	0.24%	0.25%

Data from New Castle County Vocational–Technical School District (August, 2001).
Performance Indicators: Report Card for the School Year 2000–2001.

Faculty assumptions and analyses of how Hodgson students learn and do not learn have contributed to Hodgson's commitment to integrate academic and vocational education and to make school "a caring, cooperative school community which encourages all students to become self-disciplined, productive citizens through quality teaching, integrated learning and applied technology" (Hodgson *Mission Statement*, 1990, 1998). While Hodgson's approach has yielded impressive results in attendance, graduation, dropout, employment, postsecondary school enrollment, and school suspension rates, comparisons with the two other New Castle District high schools demonstrate that it makes a particularly significant difference in students' continuing education rate and postgraduation employment rate (see Table 1.1). Additionally, Hodgson's continuing education rate is 15% higher than the U.S. average for vocational education graduates in U.S. public high schools.[2] It nearly tripled shortly after the 1992 inception of school-

[2] Levesque, K., Lauen, D., Teitelbaum, A., Alt M., & Librera, S. (2000). *Vocational Education in the United States: Toward the Year 2000*. Available: http://nces.ed.gov/pubs2000/qrtlyspring/9cross/q9-1.html#H4
U.S. Department of Education, National Center for Education Statistics: High School and Beyond Longitudinal Study of 1980 Sophomores (HS&B-So: 1980/1992), "High School Transcript Study"; and National Assessment of Educational Progress (NAEP) 1990 and 1994 High School Transcript Studies.

based academic reforms, when only 25% of graduates went on to post-secondary education institutions.

A HIGH SCHOOL FOR NEW ENGLISH LANGUAGE LEARNERS

International High School at LaGuardia Community College began in 1985 as a New York City Board of Education and City University of New York collaboration to pair community colleges with high schools. A partner in this collaboration, International is also a member of a 15-year-old national network of Middle College high schools and community colleges. Because the collaboration, known as the Middle College High School Project, aims to provide *at-risk students* with access to higher education, International's students can take college courses along side of LaGuardia Community College students and obtain both high school and college credits. For International High School students, 100% of whom are immigrants and new English language learners, access to college and opportunities to demonstrate their achievement through authentic performance in college courses contravenes their not uncommon failing scores on the City University's English language entrance exam. Ordinarily failure on the English exam, which claims to be a performance predictor, would deny them admission to college.

Similarly to Hodgson, International's commitments are based on its particular students and what the school wants them to learn: the "linguistic, cognitive, and cultural skills necessary for [students'] success in high school, college, and beyond" (International High School, 1985). The school aims to prepare them for a successful new life in their new land. International aligns their educational goals with particular pedagogical commitments that form the school's professional standards of practice, which teachers are expected to implement and by which they support, evaluate, and grant or deny tenure to one another. These practices include an interdisciplinary, thematic, activity-based approach to curriculum, collaborative learning, and teaching; an ESL method for English language acquisition; performance assessments; and heterogeneous ability and interage grouping.

Located in the industrial section of Long Island City in the borough of Queens and within view of the mid-Manhattan skyline, International is situated on the boldly designed, converted-factory campus of LaGuardia Community College. Offices and many classrooms are squirreled into windowless cubbyhole rooms along a couple of dimly lit, gray-green basement corridors. Glass cases displaying students' artwork and trophies celebrate student and school achievements. Along these corridors, multinational and multiracial groups of students laugh, chitchat, and hang on to each other as they travel to class not far from the enviably neat and organized, closet-sized and windowless office of Principal Eric Nadelstern, where the photographs of International's first graduating class are prominently displayed.

Beyond their basement quarters, International's students have access to the college's spacious, well-appointed gymnasium, modern science and computer laboratories, and well-stocked art rooms where most art, math, science, and physical education classes are held. Additionally, students use the college library, TV studio, cafeteria, auditorium, other large spaces, and recreation areas including an Olympic-sized swimming pool. Since the college campus remains open until 10 p.m., International's students have seven hours of additional access to school services than is typical at New York City high schools, which are officially open for only 6 hours and 20 minutes.

International's 450 students come from 54 countries, speak 39 languages, and represent a wide range of native and English language and literacy proficiencies. Their school experiences reflect broad diversity as well: many had continuous schooling in their native countries, but several have experienced interrupted schooling, and some have had very little formal education. Although the school is a citywide, 9th through 12th grade magnet, it draws its enrollment primarily from Queens. Students' ages range from 14 to 21. Forty-five percent are Latino, 30% are Asian, 22% are White, and 3% are Black. Seventy-five percent of the students qualify for free or reduced-price lunch in contrast to the New York City high school average of 45%. For many, immigration to the United States has meant the hardship of leaving behind family members—sometimes parents and siblings—in nations sometimes in turmoil—and relocating at a vulnerable time in their development, when the life circumstances of their families in their homeland may be precarious at best. In many instances students reside with relatives they barely know and are lonely for the familiarity of their home.

In order to be eligible for admission to International, students must meet all of the following criteria:

- they must be United States residents for fewer than four years,

- they must score below the 20th percentile on the English Language Assessment Battery, and
- they must be designated "at risk" by a counselor or teacher at their former school unless they are newly arrived in the United States.

For students newly arrived in the United States, the determination that a student is at risk is made by a member of the International faculty conducting admissions. International classifies students as being at risk if they show evidence of being likely to fail at or drop out of a large comprehensive high school.

Almost since its inception, International's accomplishments have received national recognition: the Council for Advancement and Support of Education's award for the Best New High School/College Collaboration in the nation; the National Council of Teachers of English (NCTE)'s award for Excellence in English/Language Arts Instruction, the NCTE designation as a Center of Excellence for At-Risk Students; the American Association of Higher Education's award for Outstanding High School/College Collaboration; a Democracy '92 grant from RJR Nabisco; and a National Academic Excellence award from the U.S. Department of Education. Although International's student body is more economically disadvantaged and less skilled in the English language than students in the average New York City high school, its record of academic success is impressively higher, as demonstrated in Table 1.2.

A REAL CHANCE HIGH SCHOOL

Sitting on an acre of one of the most expensive pieces of real estate on Manhattan's Upper East Side and surrounded by glass towers that peer down on it from across narrow streets and broad avenues is the Julia Richman Education Complex, a New York City public high school building constructed in the grand style of the pre-Depression 1920s. Known as J-REC, the complex is home to six small, autonomous schools, one of which is the Urban Academy (UA), a 9th through 12th grade, 15-year-old New York City public alternative high school for 120 racially, ethnically, culturally, socio-economically, and intellectually diverse students, who range in age from 15 to 19 and live throughout the city. They are 70% African-American and Latino, 30% White and other, and mostly working class and poor (75% are eligible for Medicaid).

Table 1.2. International High School 2001 Student Outcomes

	International HS 2000–2001	NYC Average 2000–2001
Attendance	94.9%	82.5%
Graduation Rate	95%	51.0% (*ELL: 50.9–52.4%*)
Dropout Rate	1%	20.4% (*ELL: 17.2–21.3%*)
College Acceptance Rate	94%	66.1%
4-year college	60%	52.2%
2-year college	34%	13.9%
High School Course Pass Rate*	91.7%	N/A
La Guardia Community College Courses Passed	85% (261n)	N/A
Suspension Rate	2.7%	57.7%

Data Sources: Nadelstern, N., & Boso, A. (2001). *The International High School 2000– 2001 Annual Report*; NYCBOE Website: http://www.nycenet.edu/daa/01asr/ and http://www.nycenet.edu/daa/reports/Class%20of%202001.pdf

*Represents % of students enrolled who passes all of their courses.

In order to reach the Urban Academy, students enter J-REC's immaculate, cavernous lobby with its two-story-high ceilings, creamy faux Corinthian columns, and pink marble and terra-cotta tile floors; and climb up a flight of stairs in a marble-walled stairwell festooned with student-made posters and artwork and the principal's reminders about the day's schedule, SAT exams, and dental appointments. The Urban Academy occupies J-REC's second floor, except for one separate corridor that is home to Ella Baker, a pre-K to eigth-grade school. UA classrooms and offices face the school's own spacious lobby, furnished for conversation and lounging with couches, cushioned chairs, and tables found by students on this affluent neighborhood's streets. Here during lunch, breaks between classes, and after school, students lounge, converse, work, eat, and sip drinks purchased in the lobby's vending machine. A wall map pinpoints the location of colleges attended by UA graduates, including historic Black colleges, Ivy League schools, small private institutions, and New York state and city universities. Below it, the quote of the day is scrawled on a portable blackboard, surrounded by students' comments about it. Quotes of the day reflect the principal's wry sense of humor and pleasure in presenting students with puzzles, paradoxes, and uncommon ideas: "What men value in this world is not rights but privileges" (H. L. Menken); "Experience is a comb life gives you after you lose your hair" (Judith Stern); "An idealist is one who helps the other fellow to make a profit" (Henry Ford).

Mounted on walls of UA's hallways are students' black-and-white photography exhibitions: urban street scenes, portraits of diverse women with their babies, and still lifes. Banners and plaques announce UA's awards: U.S. Department of Education's 1998 Blue Ribbon School of Excellence and 2000 New American High School and the Public Education Association's Maurice Hexter Award for Excellence in Teaching. Outside the office are photos of UA's teachers and students, a graffiti board, and a table with material about UA graduation requirements, news clippings, and course offerings. The social casualness complements the intellectual rigor of the school's academic program just as the hallway's calm fish tanks complement the excitement of students.

A former deputy superintendent has described UA as "a school where bad kids go and become good. And if they go back to their former schools, they become bad again." Some students refer to UA as their "last-chance school." Others see it as their first-chance school. Ninety percent of UA students have had at least one unsuccessful experience in one or more of 35 other high schools; 60% are transfers from comprehensive, neighborhood high schools notorious for their violence and high failure and low graduation rates; 20% come from vocational or high-performing academic public high schools such as Bronx Science; 20% are from private and parochial schools; and 10% enroll directly from junior high school. Of the high school transfers, 20% come to UA as a result of a superintendent's suspension for violence or weapons possession and 25% have been "asked to leave" their former school for reasons such as poor attendance or academic failure. The students live throughout the city. Students' family circumstances vary. Some have well-functioning, supportive families. The families of others are dysfunctional or tragic. Some without any family at all live in group homes. Some are teen parents.

Founders and codirectors Ann Cook and Herb Mack describe the students as having been "underchallenged" by their previous schools. According to Cook, a few students enrolled at UA have well-developed academic skills; most, however, arrive poorly prepared for high school work. Faculty characterize students' prior school history as combinations of behaviors such as chronic cutting, dropping out, suspension because

Table 1.3. Urban Academy 2001 Student Outcomes

	Urban Academy 2000–2001	NYC Average 2000–2001
Attendance	89%	82.5%
Graduation Rate	100%	51.0%
Dropout Rate	0	20.4%
College Acceptance Rate	97%	66.1%
4-year College	95%	52.2%
2-year College	2%	13.9%
Suspension Rate	0	57.7%

Data Sources: Urban Academy Statistics; NYCBOE Website:
http://www.nycenet.edu/daa/01asr/

of violence against another student or a teacher, failing grades, patterns of not completing assignments, and depression. About 10% have never read a book to completion. Upon entry, most lack perseverance, time management skills, or the habits of work necessary for school success.

Nonetheless, UA is committed to being a people-centered, educational community that provides its students with an imaginative and intellectually demanding college preparatory course of study through its unique brand of inquiry pedagogy practiced by all faculty members (Urban Academy Laboratory High School, 1993/1991). Teachers organize curriculum around complex and engaging, often controversial questions that can be answered from multiple perspectives. Their instruction guides students to explore these questions by seeking evidence from multiple and conflicting perspectives *and* to develop a reasoned argument expressing their own perspective–that is, their own voice. Students claim that their most powerful experience at UA is finding their own voice.

Admission to UA is by application, as it is to all New York City high schools. Particularly considering their school histories, UA students achieve at an impressive level (see Table 1.3).

ORGANIZATION, RELATIONSHIPS, AND TEACHING AND LEARNING IN SCHOOLS AS COMMUNITIES OF COMMITMENT

To understand the operation of schools as communities of commitment, the chapters that follow explore Hodgson, International, and the Urban

Academy through three lenses: organization, relationships, and pedagogy. Each chapter aims to capture compelling images, vignettes, anecdotes, and dialogue from the schools that reflect the idea of school as a community of commitment. The images, anecdotes, vignettes, and dialogue are drawn from over 10 years of study of these three schools, including observations of classrooms, meetings, and school life; interviews with faculty, students, and parents; and analysis of curriculum, student work, and performance data.

Chapter 2 explores the relationship between the schools' structure and the organizational capacity to be a community of commitment. It discusses particularly important organizational features, including school size, collegial collaboration and proximity, the opportunity structure for critical reflection and dialogue, individual and organizational growth and professional development, self-governance and shared governance, and leadership.

Chapter 3 addresses the issue of relationships and explores what powerful, caring student-teacher and professional relationships are like in schools that are communities of commitment, what characterizes them, how they work, how schools make them happen and support them, how they are used to leverage student achievement, how they influence values that inform how teachers define their role, and how they are a source for collective action that can benefit the goals and commitments of individuals and the school community. Chapter 3 in particular discusses intimacy, trust, the coupling of student resistance and teacher persistence, leveraging relationships for students' social development and academic achievement, and relationships as a source of social capital. Students' testimony illuminates how their relationships with school adults facilitate their individual growth and how, when relationships are a systemic tool for student achievement, they affect students collectively.

Chapter 4 looks at pedagogy in the three schools, in particular teaching and learning for making meaning. It explores why teaching and learning for making meaning is important; how pedagogical choices, instructional practice, and curricular decisions create a variety of learning opportunities that evoke meaning making for students, teachers, and the school community; how teaching and learning for making meaning are operationalized; how teacher knowledge and intellectual capital are constructed; as well as the correspondence between school ethos and teaching and learning.

Chapter 5 reviews the internal and external conditions that elicit the student and teacher commitment necessary for schools to be communities of commitment and analyzes the policy implications for sustainability and scalability.

Hodgson, International, and the Urban Academy are high schools that achieve success with most of their students, who are not an elite population, but rather frequently are or feel marginalized and disenfranchised for reasons of race, ethnicity, language, culture, socio-economic background, learning style or interest, and sometimes simply for being different in any way. These schools' success with their students is not accidental; rather, it is the consequence of their belief systems, values, decisions about organization and pedagogy, and their powerful commitment and sense and construction of community. This book tries to capture, illuminate and understand, and learn lessons from each school's unfolding of crosscutting elements, and how they function and interact within each school—in some ways similarly and in some ways differently. The differences in how these elements play out in each of the three schools argues against the idea that there is one best cookie-cutter model or template. It argues for schools using their individual culture, building new knowledge from their experience, making their tacit practitioner knowledge explicit and public, and respecting their own organizational complexity to build strong and effective learning communities targeted to achieving their particular educational goals for their particular students.

Although rich and successful educational environments, educators at Hodgson, International, and the Urban Academy would be the first to argue that their work is always unfinished, and that there are always enduring challenges and dilemmas to which there are more effective responses than the ones they have crafted at the moment, even though their current strategies reflect their best knowledge and effort at that given moment. As a result, these schools are always changing, continuously improving, inventing, adding, and retiring structures and mechanisms, often from their own practice; and their staff has the expectation of continuous change along with the confidence to lead and embrace it. Being their own engine of change makes these schools exciting places to work, creates an intellectually vital atmosphere for teachers, and supports a high level of work engagement.

Public schools like the three featured in this book are never easy to achieve. In the past they have received critical support from organizations like the Coalition of Essential Schools and some central office and state leaders. In the current coercive and punitive educational climate, public schools like these are even harder to achieve, and for that reason, even more important to fight for. They require skilled and courageous teaching and leadership; an unwavering belief in the possibilities of the kind of education that develops the human mind, the heart, and the spirit; and an unflinching determination and capacity to achieve it. But public schools like these are possible, and for our democracy, they are essential.

CHAPTER 2

Organizing Schools to Be Communities of Commitment

"We know what's happening to students when it's happening."

—Aaron Listhaus, Teacher at International High School

Organizational structure can reinforce or undermine a school's vision, values, and belief system and it can support or constrain those pedagogical practices that correspond to that vision and value system. School structure also can define the limits of behavior and the possibilities for education and students' achievement. Structure can make the vision more or less attainable and the school more or less capable of honoring its commitments. Structure can give a school the organizational capacity to be a community, in particular, to be a community of commitment because it can facilitate or constrain members of the school community from individually and collectively enacting the school's vision and values on a daily and routine basis so that the way business is done and the norms of practice make commitment routine, not unusual.

CREATING POSSIBILITIES

A snapshot of the Urban Academy's office in action lets us see the relationship between structure and possibility at work. The UA office is a double-sized classroom, fashioned as though it were a rabbit-warren. The desks of all staff members are nestled next to one another like a horizontal Lego block construction. Piled high with modular shelves; books and papers that spill over onto each other; and telephones, fax machines, and computers, the desks form boundaries that keep privacy in creative tension with public access. A sink, refrigerator, and coffee machine hide against a back wall next to a computer printer.

In these cluttered quarters, dyads and triads of adults and students drape themselves across desks and one another and converse intently and intensely. Pairs of teachers and students squirrel together in serious discussion over corrections on assignments, clarification of classwork, problems with an alcoholic parent, and instructions for completing financial aid forms for college. One student whines in protest against having to revise a paper one more time. Another with his head hanging low makes excuses for an assignment not yet in after two extensions. One student giggles while digging her uninvited hands into a teacher's bag of potato chips. Another casually takes a chunk of melon from a teacher's fruit salad while she is eating it. Another asks for a bite of her teacher's sandwich. Throughout, teachers share their food without batting an eyelash.

At their lockers, which line one wall of the office, students brag about teachers calling them at home late at night. Proudly, they swap stories of teachers teasing them. All of this is within earshot of UA's codirector, Herb Mack, and teachers in the office. You can see in these interactions the easy access students have to teachers in their various roles of tutor, advisor, surrogate parent, counselor, confidante, and favored adult. And in the tone of students' stories and complaints—which are laced with the hidden delight of knowing they are connected to adults who care—one can overhear the affection students feel toward their teachers.

Mack's desk, situated at the threshold of the adjacent common room, where students hang out at lunch time, where classes are held, and where the faculty meet, is a popular munching stop for students on their way to and from their lockers. Here Mack keeps Band-Aid boxes and small vitamin jars brimming with assorted candies—gummy worms, M&M's, and chocolate-coated coffee bean treats. As quickly as these sweets are gobbled up, Mack replaces them, dipping into five-pound bags of candies securely stashed in a nearby locker. In the midst of traffic around the candy, Mack conducts focused meetings in hushed tones with individual students.

Codirector Ann Cook explained that the office arrangement is not accidental, but purposeful. It regularizes the informal structure for communication among all members of the school community. The intentional placement of students' lockers in the teachers' office ensures a regular flow of students who can see and be seen by the staff. This flow creates regular and spontaneous opportunities for frequent contact. It is more difficult for teachers to be isolated and for students to get lost. Teachers can "grab" students and intervene at the threshold of trouble, before it takes root and escalates, before students fall through the cracks. Teachers can connect to colleagues and discuss their accomplishments, puzzlements, and disappointments while they are still fresh. Students, too, can share the troubles and triumphs of the day, mediate academic and social tensions, and deliver and obtain comfort.

Cook believes that the office arrangement has value beyond school. It allows students to learn what authentic adult interaction is in an intellectual community by actually seeing their teachers engage one another in spontaneous debate, collaboration, argument, negotiation, and reconciliation. Because business with the outside world is conducted in the office, students also have the opportunity to observe the ways in which empowered adults authentically engage, negotiate, and manipulate the world. On one occasion, a student listened as the UA college counselor negotiated with a college admission officer on behalf of his admission. On another occasion, two students stood by as Cook argued with the Board of Education bureaucracy over purchase orders for computers. Cook asserts that this kind of access provides UA students from traditionally marginalized groups with images and understanding of how business is done in the mainstream. Through such access, Cook claims, students have opportunities to learn the nature and strategies of empowerment.

In this snapshot we see how structure can make behavior possible. We see how the physical structure and organizational structure of something as seemingly unimportant and invisible as the school office reinforces the Urban Academy's vision of itself as:

> A people-centered educational community in which adults provide students with opportunities to learn and develop, [where] people are the most important thing [where] who we are and who we want to be drives the school, [where] individual needs, not institutional needs drive the school, [where] decisions are made around constellations of people-issues rather than external requirements. (Mack, interview, 1993)

In the way business is conducted, we see that people *are* at the center and human needs *are* driving interactions. The nature and range of the diverse interactions in the office suggest that the school community defines the purpose of school and education as the social, emotional, intellectual, and civic development of its students. And indeed, UA states that its purpose is to "educate students to become life-long learners, [to engage them as] members of an academic community, [and] help [them] become good citizens" (Urban Academy Laboratory High School, 1993). Here is an explanation of how UA intends to achieve its purpose–through students' engagement in an academic community.

The nature of the interactions we see suggests that UA values the close, caring relationships that bind a community. Adults take care of students and students depend on adults and their community. Adults allow students' regressions, but they don't release them from the responsibility to produce work. Adults push their students.

We see that there are more than the obligatory exchanges. Here there is attachment, affection, and connection. We see, by the conduct of business in this snapshot, that the Urban Academy has the organization and the habits to enact its vision, its purpose, and its values. We see that the Urban Academy is poised to be a community of commitment.

International and Hodgson Vocational–Technical high schools are also structured to be communities of commitment. They, too, envision themselves as caring communities that value human beings, and are dedicated to their students' intellectual development and preparation for active citizenship and the demands of their choices and life after high school. Each school's organization maps back onto its values, vision, belief system, and context to create opportunities for individual and collective commitment. International's organization supports its commitment to educating new English language learner immigrant adolescents and Hodgson's organization facilitates the enactment of its commitments to students who have chosen to pursue a vocational-technical education.

IMAGES OF SCHOOLS ORGANIZED
FOR COMMITMENT

Although the three schools are structured differently, they share the following set of common organizational characteristics that supports them to be communities of commitment:

- Human scale school size,
- Close working proximity of teachers who collaborate,

- Formal and informal, scheduled and unscheduled opportunities for collegial collaboration,
- Regular opportunities for critical reflection and dialogue,
- Regular formal and informal, structured and unstructured, teacher-generated and school generated opportunities for individual and organizational growth and professional development,
- Norms of self-governance and shared governance embedded in all organizational and pedagogical functions,
- Strong, nurturing, and shared leadership.

Sizing Down for Human Scale

Because commitment is contingent upon personal and collective responsibility as well as caring and close relationships among individuals and between individuals and their work, schools need to organize in ways that are propitious for the development of relationships. One of the organizational variables that most easily affords opportunities for close and caring relationships, which humanizes school, is size. It can be easier for individuals to be accessible in smaller organizations than in larger ones. Relationships between students and teachers and among peers and colleagues can develop more easily in smaller than in larger schools (Gladden, 1998; Fine, 1998; Newmann & Associates, 1996; McLaughlin, 1994; Darling-Hammond, Ancess, & Falk, 1995), where people do not and cannot know one another because bigness becomes a barrier. The relationships that develop in smaller organizations can be leveraged for improved student, teacher, and school performance. In the course of using relationships to leverage higher levels of performance, faculty can strengthen students' commitment to their work. At each of the schools, vulnerable students in particular stated over and over again that the single factor most responsible for turning them around, for improving their self-confidence and academic performance, was their relationship with a teacher or administrator.

When individual attention is possible, when individuals matter, when people issues can drive decision-making, teachers can develop work that reflects the needs and interests of the school community members. Although each of the schools differs in size, each has found ways to be "small"–to be a humane, caring, personal community in which every student and teacher can be known; where everyone matters;

where no one need be anonymous, invisible, alienated, or lost; and where communication can occur directly, immediately, and with far less complication than is typical in large and bureaucratic organizations.

Each of the three schools has small size classes of under 25, which students report increases the amount of attention they receive and the interaction they have with their teachers. At the Urban Academy, all of the students interviewed claimed that the school's smallness meant that teachers got to know students well. At Hodgson, Mike,[3] a masonry student, says, "When I need help the teachers know because I'm not trying. They sit and talk to me."

Several students at International explain that their teachers observe when students do not understand the material. One explains, "[They] come to you and explain fully so you get the ideas." As students' comments suggest, there is an intimacy in their classes that transcends verbal communication so that teachers have multiple ways of knowing how students are learning. Teachers' sensitivity to subtle clues regarding students' understanding and the opportunities they have to respond are particularly important for the progress of students who are culturally and linguistically different from the mainstream and students who are academically ambivalent, alienated, or withdrawn.

The different sizes of the three schools have called for different strategies for being "small" schools. The Urban Academy has chosen to remain small with an enrollment of 120 students. One student, who compared his experience at UA with his former very large high school, effectively illustrates the difference the small scale can make:

> I remember not being able to approach any of my teachers. If you talked to a teacher about a problem, the teacher recommended that you go to the school guidance counselor. The guidance counselor listened to you and recommended you go to the school social worker. The social worker trudged through your problem and recommended you go to the court to get taken out of your home because you had an argument with your mother. Here you sit down and tell Herb or Wally [a math teacher], and they take that into account. There's an acknowledgment of a problem and help is offered.

---

[3] Pseudonyms are used for students.

Hodgson, with 900 students, is much larger than the other two schools, but it has developed strategies for making life human scale. Most teachers have voluntarily organized into semiautonomous, interdisciplinary, grade-level core teams. This organization keeps the teacher–student ratio between 1 to 50 and 1 to 75. Students notice the higher levels of attention. A Hodgson student comments: "If you're a failure, you know that they have people to help you. For example, when I speak to Mr. Grandell [a math teacher], he sits down and explains stuff until you know what you are doing." The comments of the UA and Hodgson students illustrate how the direct approach to problem-solving, which is possible in human scale environments, lends itself to more satisfying solutions than the bureaucratic approach that large-sized environments must take.

International High School, which has 450 students, has organized and reorganized itself to be smaller by restructuring into 6 self-contained, theme-based, interdisciplinary, interage, heterogeneous ability clusters staffed by six to nine faculty members. In effect, the self-contained cluster structure has enabled International to mimic being six very small schools in which teachers and students can engage one another intensely around a curricular focus and students' social and intellectual development. International's cluster structure intentionally builds on the surrogate family paradigm. This family-like model is particularly sensitive to the unique condition of immigration, which has separated many International students from their families. Many students mention that the small size of the school has made it feel "like a family," and remark that because the school is small they feel like they have many friends.

Many of International's teachers report that the clusters' small size, coupled with their autonomy, enables teams to structure the conditions for effective teaching and learning and increase teachers' capacity to personalize education and know students well. Biology teacher Alison McCluer commented that the small size of the cluster structure increases teachers' capacity to monitor students' progress: "Because we're small, [we] keep track of how students do." Both Herb Mack and Eric Nadelstern, principal of International, comment that every student is connected to at least one teacher and that these connections safeguard against students falling through the cracks.

The restructuring at International and Hodgson has occurred through a pattern of fits, starts, retreats, and starts again rather than as a smooth linear path. International adopted its present structure in 1996, 11 years after its creation and three years after its first restructuring. Except for its 70-minute periods and a trimester year, International was initially organized as a traditional high school, where students were individually programmed and traveled from class to class. Each restructuring has aimed to make International more intimate in order to improve students' achievement.

The impetus and model for International's most recent restructuring and current organization came from a teacher. David Hirschy, an experienced and once traditional physics teacher, proposed the creation of a self-contained, theme-based, interdisciplinary cluster in order to increase students' access to physics. Since students claimed that their inadequate math backgrounds discouraged them from taking physics courses, Hirschy proposed the interdisciplinary cluster in order to couple physics with math. He was also eager to capture the excitement of the kindergarten students he observed in his wife's classroom. Four colleagues—an assistant principal, an English teacher, a Physical Education teacher, and a Math professor on the faculty of LaGuardia Community College, with which International is affiliated—joined Hirschy's experiment with the new organizational and instructional structure, which was christened the Motion Program. Throughout the Motion course, Motion teachers met together regularly to collaboratively plan and problem-solve. They took collective responsibility for their teaching and students' learning and performance. After two cycles, student attendance in the Motion Program consistently surpassed the school's average. Hirschy and colleagues noticed that students sustained more in-depth and longer periods of engagement in class projects than their non-program counterparts, and none failed. All Motion teachers concurred that the performance of their Motion students surpassed that of their previous students in noncluster classes. These results are consistent with Lee & Smith's (1996) findings that cooperative and collaborative teaching-learning environments produce higher levels of student achievement.

Hirschy shared the Motion Program results with the faculty, and Nadelstern proposed restructuring the school on the Motion paradigm. The faculty rebuffed his proposal. The following year, when the Motion faculty presented sustained results coupled with student presentations and samples of student work, the faculty agreed to Nadelstern's proposal to restructure, but "not just yet." By the third year, a majority of the faculty voted to restructure into self-contained, theme-based, interdisciplinary clusters. Nadelstern then approached the faculty to adopt a year-long schedule with one group of students and was rebuffed again for 2 years, after which the faculty agreed to the yearlong schedule.

Hodgson, too, has restructured in phases beset with fits and starts. Initially a shared-time vocational center, in 1986 Hodgson was converted into a traditionally structured, full-time vocational-technical high school. At that time, explained Principal Dr. Steven H. Godowsky, the school had a nine-period day and students were streamlined into five tracks: advanced placement, college preparatory, vocational, general, and special education. After Godowsky arrived in 1989, he and a core group of faculty began a course of change to raise expectations for students and focus more on their learning needs. A number of district- and state-level initiatives catalyzed and then guided their efforts to transform the school. These included a districtwide voluntary desegregation initiative; "key practices" of the Southern Regional Education Board (SREB) that advocated for increased academic learning opportunities for vocational students and increased academic and vocational curricular integration; the Delaware Re-Learning initiative, which enabled Hodgson to join the Coalition of Essential Schools, which also emphasized intellectual development; and the decision of faculty to formally acknowledge their school as a caring, cooperative community committed to integrated academic and vocational education. Although the resulting 30+ reforms adopted by the school to enact this vision had the support of the majority of the staff, there remained a small but constant residue of resistors. According to Special Education English teacher Carolyn Steinwedel and Carpentry teacher Dave Lutz, differences in core values caused the opposition to reforms. Godowsky believes that the reforms generated resistance because they trespassed on self-imposed boundaries set by faculty for their roles. What it means to teach, what it means to teach in a vocational-technical school with an academic commitment, and what it means to teach at Hodgson came into question. Previously no one had to ask these questions. Not only the questions, but their insistence on being asked, gnawed away at some once-comfortable niches. In order to promote support for restructuring, advocates used their collegial relationships to persuade resistant colleagues, developed faculty committees to address the concerns fueling the resistance, and, like International, publicly compared students' learning outcomes pre- and post-reforms. As a result, reforms have progressed and an environment of continuous improvement is sustained.

Spatial Relations

Like the Urban Academy, the organization of space at International and Hodgson is instrumental to the implementation of the schools' vision, values, and practices and to building commitment. At the Urban Academy not only do staff share an office, but they share classrooms. Space sharing at the Urban Academy in conjunction with the school's small size increases the opportunities for encounters among individuals and thereby the amount of time faculty have to get to know one another and one another's practice. Sharing space helps to transcend the teacher isolation and the value of privatization typical in most schools and contributes to the faculty's sense of community.

At International the use of space strengthens cluster cohesion. The rooms for each of the interdisciplinary clusters are often contiguously assembled in *cul de sac* corridors. Teachers mention that this close physical proximity to their team members enables them to easily visit one another's classrooms. As a result, they get to know how their colleagues teach and how the students they share work in varied environments. Teachers claim that they see their students more frequently. Social Studies teacher Harold Bretstein remarks that the space arrangements increase teachers' interactions with students. English and Social Studies teacher Aaron Listhaus explains how the space arrangements keep teachers' knowledge current on students' progress and achievement:

> Because we float in and out of each other's classrooms and because we meet four hours a week generally on a formal basis, we talk about what students are doing. So there are no cracks because we talk about the students who we'd like to see performing better—what their problems are. We know what's happening to students when it's happening.

At Hodgson, teachers who work in academic clusters are in contiguous rooms so that they can team-teach and collaborate at will. The academic classroom arrangement at Hodgson also encourages cohesion among the interdisciplinary teaching teams. Being in close proximity makes cross-discipline collaboration easier and increases its occurrence.

In all of the schools, opportunities for close physical proximity with colleagues enables informal interactions to complement formal interactions. Informal interactions can occur spontaneously, on an as-need basis, freshly as issues arise so that interventions are timely, so that issues can get resolved quickly while they are manageable. At the Urban Academy, for example, when students' problems require immediate intervention, the office arrangement allows several teachers to notice and coverage is easy to arrange so that those adults with the strongest relationships can intercede while others cover their classes.

Close proximity among teaching teams encourages an ongoing conversation and knowledge-building among faculty who share students. International's Bretstein comments on the power of unplanned interactions to strengthen students' learning opportunities:

> Teachers in this team are NS, you know, 'non-stop,' on how to improve things. It goes on the phone at home. It goes on more here. Your mind is always moving. No such thing as not thinking about how to do something better.

The opportunity for such intensity strengthens professional relationships and professional community.

Governance and Self-Governance

Within each of the schools there is a strong belief that commitment is related to the opportunity for self-governance—that is, for the members of the school community to hold themselves accountable to their vision, values, beliefs, and constituencies. Within each of the schools there is a strong commitment to the belief that school self-governance benefits the school community, that education is more likely to be effective when the implementers are the policy makers, when the implementers are self- and peer-monitored, and when the implementers can take individual and collective responsibility for the process and products of education at their site.

School self-governance is not limited to administrative management or an administrative management team, although each school has an administrative management team. Self-governance is woven into the fabric of the schools. The schools have made the sphere of governance broad, to include policy formulation and implementation in the areas of organization, curriculum, instructional practices, staff hiring, support, evaluation, professional development, student admissions, assessment, promotion, and graduation. Self-governance is integral to each school's standards of professional practice and accountability system for ensuring equal access to knowledge and opportunities for students to learn and for supporting and monitoring high standards of performance for individuals and the school.

Their governance processes draw widely on faculty and students, who participate in various ways and to various degrees in every aspect of the school's operation. This broad participation promotes a broad sense of ownership and strengthens common ground and commitment. Through the governance process, the members of the school community have multiple opportunities to revisit their vision, their values, their policies, and their practices as well as their suitability and alignment. They construct and reconstruct the organization and reorganization of the school so that it corresponds more closely to their values and intentions.

Because the Urban Academy faculty is small in number, all can and do participate directly in decision-making on the policies and practices that guide the school. Decisions are made by consensus. Each week, the staff meets for 3 hours to attend to school business, which means students' problems and progress, teaching, learning, curriculum, inquiry pedagogy, and performance assessments. Instead of standing, specialized committees as the machinery of school governance, UA has adopted an informal, fluid, and organic structure for addressing problems and issues. Interested staff form study groups to investigate and problem-solve various matters as they emerge and then recommend policy to the whole staff. Staff study groups have formed to address the school's grading policy, which as a result now combines narratives and letter grades, performance-assessment policy and instruments, graduation policy and process, student admissions policy and procedure, and schoolwide curricular practices such as the initiative to create a reading culture that resulted in schoolwide reading groups. After the study group has formulated the policy recommendation, or the proposed process, or completed its charge, the study group disbands.

Urban Academy students participate in school governance and decision-making through the school's organizational tutorial system, which is analogous to academic advisories. Every student belongs to an organizational tutorial and each tutorial elects one member to participate on the Student Committee, which meets with Mack for 1 hour a week to discuss students' concerns. Issues they have discussed include school policy on graffiti, food in class, displays of sexist photographs on lockers, the consequences for lateness, school spirit, the design of school jackets, and magazines the school should order for the common room. The committee submits recommendations on school policy and practice to the staff. Occasionally its representatives attend and participate in staff meetings but leave when the faculty discuss students. Student Committee representatives report back to their tutorials and often lead them in discussions. Students also give faculty feedback on prospective teaching candidates.

International's governance process emerges from its beliefs on instruction as articulated in the school's statement of philosophy:

> The most effective instruction takes place when teachers actively participate in the school decision-making process, including instructional program design, curriculum development, materials selection, faculty hiring, staff training, and peer evaluation. (International High School, 1985)

International's shared governance structure is designed to be democratic and encourage ownership, affiliation, and voice on the part of all constituencies. Decisions are made by majority vote, although the faculty works to achieve consensus or broad-based agreement on policies.

A Coordinating Council, Staff Development Committee, Faculty Personnel Committee, and Curriculum Committee oversee the business of the school. The Coordinating Council is comprised of the school's administrators, the teachers union representative, the Parent–Teacher Association (PTA) president, the student government president, and one representative from each of the six teaching teams into which the faculty is organized. The entire school elects the chair of the Coordinating Council who, along with a past chair and the Personnel Committee chair, comprise the school's Steering Committee. The Staff Development Committee plans and oversees in-service professional development. The Faculty Personnel Committee oversees the selection of new staff members and administers the peer support and evaluation process. The Curriculum Committee coordinates the school's development of curriculum, reviews each teaching team's course offerings, course content, and instructional objectives to assure the overall coherence of the school's instructional program, its correspondence to the state's curriculum frameworks, and students' access to the coursework necessary for graduation. It guards against repetition in course content, sets rigorous standards for student performance, and oversees student assessment.

Like Mack, Nadelstern meets regularly with the student government organization to discuss students' concerns and work out solutions to grievances. On its own, the student government meets weekly under the advisement of a faculty member, sponsors activities such as talent shows, international dinners, dances, and outings that strengthen the school as a multicultural community, and discusses school policies.

Hodgson's mechanism for shared governance is its steering committee, which consists of the principal, the three assistant principals, academic department chairs, and other faculty members. Initially, any staff member interested could join the Steering Committee, but when the principal's cabinet was collapsed into the Steering Committee, a system of participant rotation was put in place. The committee is led by a chairperson who is elected on a yearly basis. As a 1998 statement of purpose explains, the Steering Committee provides a forum for exploring diverse ways for improving the school: "to serve as a catalyst to communicate ideas and policies, promote instructional best practices, and foster a school-wide tone of decency" (Hodgson *Mission Statement,* 1998).

One assistant principal asserts that "the Steering Committee looks for ways to involve everyone. This inclusive policy creates an atmosphere [in which] everyone is eager to find their niche in improving the school." Several teachers state that the Steering Committee's reputation for broad representation makes it a major mechanism for securing wide support for school policies (see Appendix, Exhibit 2).

In addition to Hodgson's Steering Committee, specialized committees oversee diverse initiatives such as math integration, technology infusion, and performance assessments. Although Godowsky and the assistant principals play a significant role on these committees, interested faculty members staff and chair them. These committees debate, develop, and recommend policy to Godowsky and the Steering Committee, which then decides on implementation. They are also one of the school's primary tools for program assessment, as teachers discuss the impact of instructional initiatives. In order to incorporate students' perspectives and interests in school policies and to encourage their ownership of school initiatives, several of the committees have student members.

Lutz and Steinwedel explain that student involvement creates the expectation for students to have a voice and greater ownership in their school. When Hodgson students were asked to assess the school's implementation of its mission, students wanted to know why they had been excluded from its construction. Although they endorsed the mission statement, they noted that the school's implementation of it was incomplete. They discussed their concerns about relationships and communication with teachers, the nature of their learning experiences, and issues of equity. They wanted teachers and students to develop their understanding of the student population's cultural and intellectual diversity to ensure that all students would feel more accepted. They discussed the stress caused by academic demands. Steinwedel described one event in the students' school assessment process:

> [The staff] met with small groups of students and we started
> to pick apart the mission statement and look at ourselves
> very closely. We asked, "Are we doing this?" We say that we
> want a caring, cooperative community. We're saying,
> "You've seen our mission statement. How are we doing?
> How do you feel about this? How can we improve this? Are
> we getting there? What can we do to get there?"

One assistant principal recounted the conditions students described for stronger implementation of the mission, including their disappointment at being excluded from its development:

> Kids responded on mission statement that we need more
> communication between students and faculty and more days
> where students and teachers can talk. Some said they needed
> to be weaned into the process of small group discussion–
> hadn't done it before. They wanted to know why the faculty
> wrote the mission statement without them.

As we see from the responses of Hodgson students, commitment is not a sometimes thing. Committed community membership generates the expectation for regular, active participation in decision-making and requires inclusion of all constituencies to be sustained.

Students at International also took offense at their exclusion from the faculty's decision to restructure the school into clusters. Within 6 weeks of the implementation of the new self-contained cluster structure and a new grading policy, several juniors and seniors organized a formal protest to rescind it. They objected to what they perceived as the new organization's social and academic constraints. Many students felt the new cluster structure constrained their freedom and changed the pattern of their social life, limiting their daily interaction to under 100 students. Under the previous school organization, students could encounter many more of their peers. One student commented, "Like last year we had an opportunity to meet everyone in the school. When we walk down the hall, I'm like, 'Hi, hi, hi.' I know everyone. But this year, I have to stick with the same people." Many boys in particular resented the new structure's obstacles to meeting new female students.

In some instances, students felt academically short-changed. Since not all clusters offered courses they wanted, for example, economics, they were limited to the few courses offered within the cluster. Under the former system, students felt they had more and diverse courses from which to choose. A student-planned strike in which students would have left classes to walk out of school was averted by a series of meetings between student leaders, Nadelstern, and teacher leaders. Faculty respected the protest by permitting students to discuss their concerns during class time. They dignified students' responses by listening sympathetically to them. They protected the legitimacy and integrity of the conflict by sharing students' feedback with their colleagues and Nadelstern, by being channels of communication, and by participating in discussions to resolve the problem.

Faculty and students negotiated, with the result that additional college and elective courses outside the cluster structure were offered to seniors. But many juniors, whose concerns were not accommodated to their satisfaction, remained resentful despite Nadelstern's assurances that they would have an additional year and a half to adapt to the new structure and would have access to those courses then not available to them. Full student acceptance of the new structure occurred only after the juniors graduated.

Organizing the Instructional Program for Commitment to the Work

The privatization of practice common in most schools makes teachers' commitment to their work a private and personal matter. Within one school, it is not unusual for teachers to demonstrate a range of commitment (or lack of it) to their work, from those whose devotion becomes legendary to those who are waiting out their time. Similarly, the culture of privatization makes it not uncommon to find within one school a broad range of and even conflicting values and beliefs about education, pedagogy, the students, how they learn, and the role of the teacher. Although a school may have a vision statement, often its only manifestation is on paper.

Even when a school intends to be a community of commitment, it is not for the wishing. It needs to structure time and opportunities for commitment to be an organizational function and to function organizationally. There must be an infrastructure to support commitment-making and commitment-keeping. The school structure must provide faculty and students with time and formal and informal opportunities to make commitments to their work, to define and engage in work that is meaningful to them, to have control over the conditions and decisions that govern their work, to assess their work, and to make changes in it.

Commitment to the work has several dimensions. For teachers, it means a belief in the organization and intention of their content and their pedagogy, to students' learning, and to the connection among these variables. What students describe as teacher caring and dedication to them and their subject area are also manifestations of teacher commitment. Teachers stay late, they help students with their personal problems, they encourage them with passion and humor, and they persist to elicit student progress and achievement. Students notice their teachers' behavior, their dedication, and their passion for their teaching and content, and it makes a difference in students' willingness to persist in their struggles to succeed, particularly when they have been easily discouraged and have had bouts of school disappointment and failure (Ancess, 1994; Darling-Hammond, Ancess, & Falk, 1995).

Students' commitment is manifest in their willingness to authentically rather than perfunctorily engage in learning activities, to take responsibility for their assignments, to take ownership for what they produce, to persevere in the face of obstacles, and to persist in the demands and struggles for quality performance. Discussing her Senior Project, "How to Produce a Full Crown and Bridge Roundhouse," Hodgson dental assisting student Christina explained her struggles:

> I can't stress the patience you need to do this work. I don't
> know how many times I nearly threw in the towel. I've
> learned how to deal with my own self-control. I've learned

how to be by myself. I learned I can't let my personal problems get in the way of the Senior Project because the Senior Project goes on. When I had a problem I had to be able to open my mouth and say what was wrong.

Christina spent 153 hours and 17 minutes on her product and 205 hours and 45 minutes on the whole project.

One of Christina's teachers said, "She did all her own drawings and caught herself in her own errors."

Her advisor commented, "She stayed after school to work on the project." Godowsky delights in overhearing students' cafeteria conversations about their Senior Project sacrifices. They refuse dates and parties so that they can meet their deadlines.

Each of the schools has organized its instructional program to support teachers' and students' commitment to each other and to the work. They have constructed a pedagogical framework in which to structure the organizational variables of schedules, time, teacher assignments, course scope and sequence, and student access (course assignments) in ways that reflect their vision and values for teaching, learning, and student progress and achievement. The Urban Academy has organized its instructional program as though it were a single class of students with several teachers, all of whom reshuffle and then subdivide each semester into the variety of courses teachers teach and students select. The continual reshuffling generates multiple opportunities for multiple forms of access and interaction among the various members of the school community. Because this organization enables students to encounter almost all UA teachers and in most cases for several courses, teachers can get to know students, how they work, what their strengths, weaknesses, and interests are, how to motivate them, and how to support higher levels of performance.

UA's organization is less like a typical high school than a college. The intention of the college-like organization, explain Mack and Cook, is to ensure that course needs—that is, what UA wants to accomplish with students—drive school structure, not the reverse. For example, if a course plans for students to spend time in museums and libraries, it can be scheduled for 2 1/2 hours two afternoons a week without disrupting the school or other classes. Courses are not scheduled to meet daily, but several times a week (see Appendix, Exhibit 1). The time frames for classes vary from 55 minutes to 2 1/2 hours in order to accommodate the pedagogical needs of teachers, the learning needs of students, course ambitions, and logistical requirements such as time for students to spend in museums and libraries. Throughout the day, breaks give students time to socialize and snack. As the ages, ability, and class standings of students in college courses vary, so in UA's classes there is heterogeneous and interage grouping.

Students enroll in courses in a college-like process. At the beginning of each semester students register for courses by choosing among a variety of offerings published in that term's course catalog. The courses students choose are guided by their personal goals, their interest, and UA's graduation requirements. After considering students' preferences, the staff assigns students to courses on the basis of academic, social, and individual student needs, group chemistry, class size, and state and school graduation requirements. One student who had dropped out in his former, very large high school comments on UA's commitment to students' intellectual engagement: "If there's really a class you want here there's no reason why you shouldn't be able to get it. If you can't get it then you will leave feeling there was a good reason for it." Mack and Cook claim that UA's schedule has encouraged responsible behavior on the part of students because they are treated as adults, and it has provided UA with flexibility in teachers' programs and roles.

International's cluster system is also organized to elicit teacher and student commitment by building on their interests, personal and professional goals, strengths, and passions while simultaneously meeting state and school requirements for graduation, satisfying the school's pedagogical and social justice ethos, and preparing students for their future. The six- to nine-person faculty team that staffs each of International's 6 year-long, self-contained, thematic interdisciplinary clusters is responsible for 75–100 students who are divided into three or four classes that are called *strands.* Strands range in size from 20 to 25 students. Each team is responsible for the total educational and social needs of students in their cluster and has the autonomy and authority to make decisions about scheduling, students' assignment to classes, curriculum, instructional strategies, assessment, discipline, and the social needs of students.

The opportunity for teachers to select those colleagues with whom they want to team and to develop theme-based clusters and courses that merge their discipline-based interests and passions with students' learning needs, state and school graduation requirements, and the school's vision, values, and learning goals encourages faculty commitment to the school mission. The six faculty teams designed and developed the six 2-part theme based clusters that comprise the school's instructional organization: "Motion: Visibility" and "Invisibility"; "It's Your World" and "Conflict/Resolution"; "Beginnings" and "Structures"; "American Dream" and "American Reality"; "21st Century" and "Crime and Punishment"; and "The World of Money" and "The World Around Us." The team members also design and develop the four to six theme-related courses they teach.

The clusters offer a total of eight discrete math courses, eight discrete science courses, and two courses that integrate math and science. Topics in the science courses include Physics, Biology, Chemistry, Geology, Anatomy, Evolution, and Genetics. The Math courses offered include Algebra, Geometry, Precalculus, Probability, and Statistics. The content of the humanities courses is designed to be responsive to the conditions of new English language learning and immigration. Although the cluster courses reflect their themes and particular teachers' interests, they prepare students to meet the state requirements for graduation. For example, "Linguistics" and "Multi-cultural Creation Myths," two English/Language Arts courses in one cluster, require students to compare and contrast the structure of their own language to the structure of other students' languages and to English.

Over the course of their 4 years at International, students select four of the six clusters and are assigned on the basis of their choices. Within the clusters they take required courses and also choose courses. Within classes, they have choices of projects and groups in which to work. At each turn, teachers reinforce the idea that these choices represent opportunities for commitment. Teacher Ronni Green explains the relationship between the student choice and student commitment at International: "Kids have a great deal to say in this school. They make a lot of choices and they make commitments, and they have a lot to say about what it is they want to get out of their education. And they're encouraged to make commitments to that."

Hodgson's efforts to restructure its instructional program for faculty and student commitment reflect the triple challenge of a vocational-technical school that aims to support academic development for academically ambivalent students in conjunction with vocational and technical education, and the integration of both. Hodgson also has the challenge of eliciting the commitment of conventionally independent and separate academic and vocational faculties in order to develop academic and vocational integration. To approach these challenges, Hodgson used three organizational strategies: (1) voluntary core academic teams, (2) block scheduling, and (3) grassroots instructional design.

In order to strengthen students' commitment to the school's academic component, Hodgson's ninth grade is organized into interdisciplinary core teams, each of which consists of three courses: English/Language Arts, World Cultures, and Biology. Each core team of teachers teaches one group of students and is block-programmed for four periods for the three courses so that teams have the flexibility and time to implement curricular and pedagogical innovations that can strengthen students' academic engagement and performance, such as project work, enrichment, more intensive reading, and more in-depth instruction in academic coursework.

The teams are self-governing and have the authority and flexibility to group and regroup students according to their learning needs and styles, which focus faculty and students on the learning tasks and on the collective collaboration of faculty and students that is necessary for the successful completion of the tasks. Teachers, who have a common meeting time during which they plan and assess their program and students' progress and achievement, frequently use an interdisciplinary thematic approach to instruction, especially for their intensive writing program which is taught across the three content areas. Although students initially complain about the seriousness of the writing program, this program sets the foundation for the skills they will need to produce the reports and research papers required in the upper grades. Many attribute the school's high ranking on the Delaware statewide tenth-grade writing test to the instructional cohesion of Hodgson's ninth-grade core teams.

In order to encourage higher levels of student performance, Hodgson accommodates students' academic learning needs through the strategy of block scheduling for core clusters and all 10th- and 11th-grade academic courses. There are semester-long 90-minute classes for courses that previously were allocated 45 minutes. Block scheduling provides teachers with the flexibility to adjust time periods to suit particular teaching and learning variables in ways that can make instruction more meaningful. According to Hodgson's catalogue of "best practices," the block schedule encourages academic commitment by providing "more instructional time for the student, less subjects to concentrate on at a single time, and a new schedule after the second semester" (Hodgson Vocational–Technical High School, 1998). Math teacher Mark Grandell asserts that the block provides the flexibility to give students projects and frees teachers from the time constraints that he believes encourage reliance on textbooks and lectures, strategies that do not work for Hodgson students.

The vocational-technical program is structured for students to make a commitment to a career concentration in which they can ultimately specialize and prepare for the world of work. Students first explore Hodgson's diverse career options through the ninth-grade Exploratory Program, in which every 22 days students rotate through different career clusters of courses so that they are prepared by the last marking period to choose a major that interests and engages them. They are then placed in their first-choice career program. In the 10th and 11th grades students take four periods of vocational courses, one of which is a technology course related to their vocational major. This new requirement acknowledges the increasingly important role of technology in the trades. In 11th grade, students participate in internships that help them develop their vocational, technical, and academic skills at external sites that range from a local banks to various companies in the construction trades. Students also participate in job shadowing and mentorships with local businesses.

In order to promote faculty commitment to Hodgson's academic and vocational education integration initiatives, the school's academic and vocational teachers collaborated to design and develop them. Academic and vocational education teachers were given time to collaboratively design and develop both the professional development that would enable them to implement integration initiatives as well as student curriculum and course work. One major initiative produced by these collaborations is the Senior Project, which requires all seniors to produce a product from their shop major, a related research paper, and an oral presentation that extends and synthesizes their learnings. A faculty committee constructed the Senior Project from successful school practices, field tested it over time, and revised it in response to formal and informal teacher and student feedback (Darling-Hammond, Ancess, & Falk, 1995).

Once the integration initiatives are in place, teachers create class structures that enable students to make commitments to this work. Time in Shop classes is formally allocated to support students' work on the Senior Project. The 12th-grade English course is a 90-minute technical writing class that guides students through the formulation and execution of their Senior Project research paper. Reciprocal scheduling by students and their Senior Project advisor ensures that students receive the individual time, attention, support, oversight, and pressure they need for the successful execution of all aspects of the Senior Project.

Staffing

In order for schools to sustain themselves as cohesive communities, that is, organizations that can sustain particular commitments to a common vision and set of values, they need to ensure that the beliefs and practices of community members are compatible with one another and with the school's values and intentions. Therefore, schools that intend to be communities need to exercise control over their staffing, not only in terms of who is hired to be a teacher or leader and the nature of their roles, but the conditions for continuance at the school and professional practice.

In various ways, faculty in each of the schools participates in staff hiring. At Hodgson, departmental chairs and other administrative faculty are most directly involved in hiring new faculty, but the Steering Committee establishes criteria for teachers so that new hires support the school's educational policies and practices, such as performance assessments, and are prepared to implement them. In fact, to strengthen the school's commitment to vocational and academic integration and performance assessment, the Steering Committee urged the principal to require faculty participation in the Senior Project and demand transfers for resisters.

Urban Academy faculty interview all candidates for teaching positions. Teachers observe them teach a class to assess their rapport with students, their content expertise, and their pedagogical expertise and compatibility. The faculty takes candidates to lunch to discuss their impressions of the school and to get to know them socially. Students also make recommendations to Mack and other staff. Decisions on who will be hired are made by the entire faculty at a staff meeting.

International's teacher hiring process has become the model for the New York City school system and is part of the school system's contract with the teachers union. The Faculty Personnel Committee reviews resumes of candidates, interviews them, observes them teaching, and then selects the candidate(s) most qualified for the school's needs. Teacher seniority, which once determined access to teaching positions, is subordinated to teacher qualification for particular contexts.

Because these hiring policies enable faculty to hire like-minded colleagues, they can strengthen faculty cohesion and educational coherence and thereby increase the consistency with which individual teachers apply their school's pedagogical values and practices. As Lee and Smith

(1996) discovered, the aggregate of such consistency increases students' achievement levels. Student outcomes at Hodgson, International, and the Urban Academy confirm this finding. The consistent and rigorous cross-discipline application of what one Hodgson teacher referred to as an "intense" writing program contributed to Hodgson's ranking first on the Delaware state writing exam only 2 years after the program's inception. International's consistent, cross-cluster implementation of a fail-one-course, fail-all-cluster-courses grading policy increased student course pass rates immediately. Pedagogical practice at the Urban Academy has helped former dropouts and cutters graduate high school and enroll in college at rates as high as New York City's top high schools.

The reconceptualization and redesign of staff roles also supports faculty commitment. At all three schools', staff take on multiple roles and are not bound by specialization. Faculty agree to blur some of the traditional boundaries that separate administrators and teachers. Teachers' responsibilities extend beyond instruction and administrators teach and regularly engage students in multiple ways. At the Urban Academy all faculty, including the codirectors, teach courses and assume administrative responsibilities. For example, one teacher is responsible for student admissions. Two other teachers coordinate UA's required community service program. Teachers' multiple roles provide them with opportunities to know students from different perspectives, which they share with one another and use to inform their decisions. Math teacher Wally Warshawsky, who oversees students' records, keeps track of all the courses students take and the credits they accumulate. When the staff assigns students to classes, Warshawsky provides information on the credits students need so that course assignments can take these needs into consideration. At meetings he informs his colleagues on the progress or problems of students, providing details on how particular students are doing in other teachers' classes, on which students seem consistently over time to perform best with which teachers, and on which students may need intervention because of changes in their behavior patterns. His perspective enables him to see students' patterns of performance and the data help his colleagues analyze students' needs and determine a course of action. Warshawsky's role helps UA faculty to coalesce around students and collectively focus on meeting their needs.

Since teachers in each of the clusters at International High School are responsible for the total educational and social needs of the students in their cluster, their roles are less specialized than is common in most high schools. Cluster teachers assume instructional, administrative, and student guidance functions. Although one teacher takes responsibility for cluster coordination and facilitates and prepares the agenda for the regular cluster meetings, other teachers represent their cluster on the school's various policy committees. Similarly at Hodgson, teachers in the core teams transcend the boundaries of their content area specialties and take responsibility for organizing instructional time within their common blocks, make interdisciplinary curricular and team teaching decisions, and many participate on the various policy committees that shape the school's implementation of its mission and determine its future direction. These opportunities for broad-based participation in the life of the school, for decision-making at various levels, are incentives for teachers to invest in their school by shaping it so that their values merge with the school's values and so that the school community is part of them as they are part of the school community. There is reciprocity of commitment where faculty embraces the commitments of the school, where the school embraces the commitments of faculty, and where the bonds of community are strengthened.

Leadership

Both the structure of leadership and the role of school leader are organized to encourage schoolwide commitment. As indicated by their governance structure and by the role teachers play in the design and development of their instructional program, the schools each implement a model of collaborative leadership. Nonetheless, Cook, Mack, Nadelstern, and Godowsky are strong leaders who demonstrate commitment to the vision and values of their school and who encourage and support commitment on the part of the members of their school community. Their leadership strategies for strengthening commitment to their school's vision and to the practices that will enact the vision are shaped by school context, organizational demands, and individual personality and character. And although these variables differ as the schools do, the leaders' roles and their strategies for strengthening commitment have much in common. They are catalysts for change, nurturers through struggle, community builders, managers, instructional leaders, entrepreneurs, and representatives to the public.

These leaders are often catalysts as well as participants in their school's efforts to implement their vision. To catalyze Hodgson's whole school reform, Godowsky initiated early morning and afternoon conversations on faculty-generated topics with any faculty who wanted to attend. These conversations became the forum for a core group of regulars to explore and debate the principles of the Coalition of Essential Schools (CES) and Delaware's Re-Learning Initiative, which Hodgson would eventually adopt to guide their reform (Ancess & Darling-Hammond, 1994). This conversational approach webbed out to the staff at large when the regulars, who became the critical core of reformers, individually and in friendship groups engaged more peripheral staff in discussions on reform. In order to encourage the implementation of the reforms, Godowsky supports professional development, schedule changes, and the development of staff committees to plan, oversee, assess, and modify them.

Nadelstern encourages teachers to collaborate on innovations by listening to their ideas and concerns, allocating the time and financial resources, and providing a public forum for knowledge-sharing and debate as he did with Hirschy. He pushes the staff directly, as when he urged them to adopt schoolwide the structure of the Motion Program. But he knows when to back off and when to push again. He is not intimidated or deterred by setbacks.

At the Urban Academy, where Mack and Cook share leadership responsibilities, Mack takes responsibility for internal matters and Cook takes responsibility for external matters. While there is some territorial overlapping, there is no duplication. Cook interacts with the Board of Education and external agencies and partners in the public and private sectors. She collaborates with teachers on special projects, such as the design and development of performance-based assessments, and supports their revision. Mack oversees the administration of the school as well as its instructional organization. He organizes schedules, facilitates faculty meetings, works with teachers to design and develop new courses that connect their interests and passions with student and school needs, and team teaches with novices so that they can learn the school's norms of pedagogy. Both teach courses.

These leaders provide staff with information and feedback to encourage their individual and collective commitment to and responsibility for student and organizational outcomes. Hodgson administers a variety of surveys to parents, students, and teachers to assess school satisfaction, school performance, and the efficacy of instructional initiatives such as the Senior Project. The staff reviews the results and decides upon a course of action in response to them. It was through such surveys that the Senior Project Committee developed scaffolding to more effectively support students' work on the Senior Project.

Nadelstern publishes the distribution of students' grades across clusters, students' college course-taking rates, graduation rates, attendance rates, results on state exams, and the faculty's evaluation of his own performance and recommendations for his improvement. Teachers use student outcome data to assess their own performance. When one teaching team noticed that their cluster had the highest number of student incompletes, they voluntarily assigned themselves as mentors to each student who had an incomplete, even though none of the students was any longer in the cluster. In effect, they committed themselves to working on their own time with former students in order to help them complete the work so that they could pass the cluster. Students complete course evaluations that are shared with faculty and which faculty use to revise curriculum and instruction. In fact, students contribute to the design of these evaluations. At the Urban Academy, Cook conducts exit interviews with graduating students who assess the strengths and weaknesses of their experience at the school. The feedback is shared with the staff, who uses it to make programmatic revisions.

In each school, the leaders support the development of professional community as a strategy for strengthening teachers' commitment to their work. There are multiple opportunities for professional development, oftentimes provided by colleagues. English chair MaryAn Scarbrough believes that Hodgson's most powerful professional development has been what the staff itself has designed and provided (Ancess & Darling-Hammond, 1994). At the Urban Academy, less experienced teachers have opportunities to team teach with more experienced teachers, including the codirectors, each of whom, like other Urban faculty, has designed courses that each then teaches. Through International's peer support system, teachers form dyads and triads where they observe each other teach and review each other's curriculum. International also finances external professional development, which has involved teachers in Uri Triesman's Mathematics Innovations and the American Social History Project. In all of the schools, teachers who work together, either on projects, in study groups, or in clusters are regularly scheduled for common meeting time.

To support students' commitment to the school, the leaders of each of the schools are regularly accessible to and involved with students individually and in structured groups such as the student government. Steinwedel remarks about Godowsky: "If there are three students and one teacher waiting to see him, the teacher will probably not be the first one who goes into that office, which is great. There's an open-door policy." Hodgson students mention the school's efforts to promote positive behavior. One said: "They try to get you involved in a lot of school activities like student liaison where you get to talk about everything that goes on in the school."

Cook meets individually with all students who need social services and personally negotiates with city and Board of Education bureaucracies to secure them. Mack seeks out interactions with almost every student to find out how they are doing. He regularly meets with students for whatever reason they want to meet. Many students briefly stop by his desk in the office for quick reassurance. Others meet with him to solve personal and academic problems. Yet others who are in his course meet with him for help with their assignments. Still others stop by to debate and tease. He walks into classes first thing in the morning and after lunch to note which students are present and absent. When teachers do not submit their period-by-period attendance lists, Mack "bugs [them] about which kids are not in class." He shares these lists with the teachers during the day so that they have immediate information about who may have cut. Two students remarked that they and their parents were very impressed that the head of their school actually called them at home when he was at his home. They had not expected or previously experienced this level of commitment.

Nadelstern explains that the cluster structure has influenced the structure of leadership, making him and his assistant principal, Ruthellen Weiner, more accessible to support students' intellectual development. Because they now deal, says Nadelstern, "with six teams rather than fifty individual teachers," they assess the work of teams and the capacity of their interdependency to produce effective classroom instruction. With their supervisory responsibilities streamlined, Nadelstern and Weiner join clusters as teacher colleagues in order to model effective pedagogy for teams with less experienced teachers and to contribute their knowledge and skills in team conversations. Such intervention provides students with access to effective teaching and teachers with access to professional development designed to improve the delivery of services they are providing to their students. It reinforces the school's commitment to teaching and learning as its primary responsibility.

Professional Development and Professional Community

In schools that are communities of commitment, professional development and professional community are organized to be mutually reinforcing. This interdependency increases the capacity of individual faculty and the school as a community to be accountable to its broader purposes and to enact its commitments. Faculty collaboration and reflective dialogue and debate clarify and reinforce shared values and norms, focus faculty on students and their learning, and provide a window into colleagues' practice. All of these activities constitute both professional community (Louis, Kruse, & Marks, 1996) and powerful professional development. Faculty learn from their practice and feed their learning directly back into it.

Most professional development at the schools is organized to build and build on professional community, teachers' knowledge, successful practice, experience, and collaboration. Although teachers participate in external professional development, such as the American Social History Project at International High School, time is scheduled for internal, faculty-generated professional development, which simultaneously reinforces professional community. Teachers on Hodgson's Senior Project Committee were given time to develop the Senior Project. Self-selected Hodgson teachers were given time to develop the 11th-grade "American Experience" course, which integrates Social Studies and English/ Language Arts. Math and Shop teachers were given time to develop the Mathematics Integration Initiative, which aims to improve students' understanding of and performance in mathematics by integrating mathematics and vocational curriculum.

Math teacher Janet Ryer noted how the Math Integration Project connected professional community, professional development, and increased student learning opportunities: "It helped the integration of voc and academic education because it built bonds between teachers who would have never otherwise interacted." The organization for the mutual reinforcement of professional community and professional development increases the school's capacity to honor its commitments, in the case of Hodgson, to improve students' academic performance by effectively integrating vocational and academic education. Hodgson's allocation of time for Math and Shop teachers to get to know one another, to visit one another's classes, and to develop professional relationships as a strategy for integrating math and vocational education curriculum also couples professional development with professional community.

The Urban Academy initiates each semester with an event called "The Curriculum Project," for which the entire faculty collaboratively selects a theme and a corresponding broad-based question for pursuit. Collectively, the faculty plans the project around the question and theme. Then school engages in the project. The project is at once both a valid learning experience for students and professional development to enhance teachers' capacity to develop and implement inquiry curriculum in accordance with the UA's norms of practice. At the conclusion of the project, the faculty meets to evaluate it and distill lessons for practice. Collectively they assess their teaching and students' learning against their indicators for inquiry learning and school as an academic community. During the planning phase and the 2-week implementation of the project, faculty not only observe one another planning instruction, but they also see one another's implementation. As they strengthen their common language and common imagery of practice, they clarify their values and norms.

In each school, professional development occurs informally and formally but always in connection with the professional community and the school's commitments. Examples of the informal opportunities for teacher learning have been mentioned previously: the encounters in the Urban Academy Office or on the phone at home among International's teachers. Formally organized professional development includes initiatives such as UA's Curriculum Project, but each of the schools also schedules regular meetings at which faculty, either as a whole or as clusters, critically reflect on their practice, problem-solve, and plan collaboratively for instruction and student interventions. The regularity and routine of these meetings serves the important purpose of reinforcing the school's core values, shared norms of practice, and the faculty's sense of collective responsibility for student and organizational outcomes. These regular meetings, the time blocks for which range from 1 to 3 hours weekly, strengthen the school community and the capacity of its members individually and collectively to enact its commitments. Just as teachers teach together within a collegial structure, they learn together within a collegial structure of meetings.

A fragment of a meeting of the Beginnings/Structures cluster provides a snapshot of the iterative dynamic of professional development and professional community at International High School. In a small, windowless room, eight faculty members sit around trapezoid tables. Charlie Glassman, the team facilitator, passes out the agenda. Since

Beginnings/Structures has adopted a case management approach to students, the staff has a list of students to discuss. They begin with one student, Grisel, discussing their experiences with what they called "her acting out":

> "She comes late."
> "She disappears from class."
> "She hangs out."

Math-Science teacher Simon Cohen strongly recommends a parent conference. Biology teacher Alison McCluer and English-Linguistics teacher Anthony DeFazio respond that they have had one and discuss their meeting with Grisel's mother, at which she confessed that she did not know what to do. Linguistics, Art, and French teacher Elise Rivin asks, "Why is Grisel doing work in my class?" Teachers ask for more details. Rivin describes Grisel's projects in her Art class. The teachers make a distinction between the verbal and visual demands of the classes in which she is not performing. Cohen recounts how when Grisel was in his class, he explained what she would have to do to succeed, and she accepted his terms. The teachers conclude that they need more information in order to understand Grisel's behavior and decide what to do.

Glassman suggests a group meeting with Grisel. At group meetings, faculty collectively confront students with their behavior and then develop a plan for improvement with them. Beginnings/Structures teachers report that students are powerfully affected by being confronted by all of their teachers. The team agrees to a group meeting.

The team brings up another student, Vlad. Again they describe his behavior. Rivin complains that Vlad is handing in new work now at the end of the term. Even though Vlad's efforts have come late, DeFazio defends them. Cohen asserts that limits need to be set so that students submit work on time and come to class on time. Glassman mediates with a question: "What tactic can we take that might be successful so that Vlad gets credit for class? How can we support him?"

Cohen suggests the team meeting strategy. He believes that the faculty needs to encourage him to produce to his capacity. He opposes letting students set all the terms. Glassman responds, "We do that. We respond to kids."

DeFazio remarks, "We're making progress. Vlad started off as someone we thought we'd lose completely. He comes to class."

Social Studies teacher Aaron Listhaus concurs, "When he comes to class his thinking and comments move the class."

Glassman returns to limits: "I agree with Simon. We have bottom lines. We have bottom lines and we enact them in a humane manner."

Cohen pursues the issue of limits: "At what point do we decide that kids' influence on the school is not viable?"

Glassman responds, "We support kids to mature. That's our job."

Skipping over Glassman's comment, DeFazio rejoins in response to Cohen's implicit counterargument on Vlad, "We disagree. I think he's improved."

DeFazio makes a recommendation: "We should ask him, 'How can we get some tangible work out of you in a timely fashion?'"

In this fragment, we see how organization can support the habits of collaborative problem-solving to improve students' performance. Team members' solutions draw on practices that have succeeded previously and reveal that they have a common experience and knowledge base. The subtext of the meeting suggests that team members struggle with enduring differences between their personal norms and interpretations and the school community's norms for student behavior. They struggle with competing priorities generated by the values and norms regarding students' behavior. They struggle with the tension between the individual good and the common good.

Explicitly they have revisited the school's core values about adult responses to students' behavior and come to a temporary clarification. They have taken collective responsibility for their students. Implicitly they have enacted the school's commitment to collaboration, to teachers' taking collective responsibility for the total education of students, and to coupling the demands for student performance with effective supports. As teachers leave this meeting with the expectation of more effectively responding to challenging students and improving their performance, the mutual reinforcement of professional community and professional development becomes visible. Despite differences, the community does not unravel.

CONCLUSION

These images of organization at the Urban Academy, International High School, and Hodgson Vo-Tech illustrate how structure can help schools be communities of commitment, how organization can help schools keep the promises of their vision, how structure and organization can release faculty to implement their own and their school's beliefs about teaching and learning, and how they can support effective teaching practice and improved student learning and achievement. Important organizational elements shared by the schools include:

- Human-scale organization
- Small-size classes
- Close physical proximity among teachers who share students
- Strong, hands-on leaders who are directly accessible to and involved with students and teachers
- Distributed and collaborative leadership
- Self-governance
- Shared policy- and decision-making
- Student participation in school governance
- Opportunities for regular teacher team and faculty meetings
- Deprivatization of teaching
- Infrastructure to support commitment-making and -keeping
- Self-staffing
- Diffuse teacher roles
- Professional development that supports professional community.

These anecdotes and images illustrate how organization can help schools be credible and accountable institutions that are responsive and responsible. We see how organizational structures can facilitate the correspondence of vision, values, and practice so that they are mutually reinforcing. We see how organizational mechanisms monitor that correspondence, so when it falls out of balance, the schools have the capacity to recalibrate, to self-correct. Organizing for commitment has enabled these three schools to be in tune with themselves and with the promises they have made to their constituencies.

The schools also have the will to be in tune with themselves and their promises. And therein lies the catch. While organizational structure makes commitment possible, it by no means makes it inevitable. Commitment requires individual and collective will. This includes the willingness of community members to make their beliefs and their practice public and open to scrutiny; the willingness to hold themselves accountable for the alignment between their promises, their practices, and their results; the willingness to collaborate, negotiate, and tolerate the enduring tensions of living and working with others; and the willingness to embrace individual and collective responsibility–that is, the steadfast belief that, regardless of circumstances, it is always the faculty and the school's responsibility to commit and recommit themselves to finding the way to get their students to learn.

Schools organized to be communities of commitment can unite the individuals who comprise the school so that the school is a cohesive organization, so that the divisions between individuals and their school dissolve, so that the individuals who comprise the school are in fact their school. By organizing a school to be a community of commitment, the boundaries between faculty and their school can become permeable– new ground can be broken, new entry points opened, and new pathways crossed. Faculty and students can become the school. There can be a fusion, a connection, a bonding where school is not just a place where people spend time. Then there can be more than buy-in. There can be exchange, attachment, and bonding among people with their work, their school, and the young people's futures.

CHAPTER 3

Caring Relationships: The Main Thing

"Caring is the main thing. You can't get educational until you get personal."

—a student

"This place hurts my spirit," says a high school student in *Voices from the Inside: A Report on Schooling from Inside the Classroom* (Institute for Education in Transformation, 1992, p. 11), an intensive study of four diverse schools in southern California.

Human relationships, the report goes on to explain:

> May be one of the two most central issues in solving the crisis inside schools. . . . Relationships dominated all participant discussions about issues of schooling in the U.S. . . . Relationships between students and teachers seem to dominate students' feelings about school. . . . Students, over and over again, raised the issue of care. (pp. 13, 19)

The long reach and powerful grasp of caring relationships in schools is well documented in close to 70 years of education research. Darling-Hammond (1997), McLaughlin (1994), Lee, Bryk, & Smith (1993), and Waller (1932) found that teacher-student affective bonds influence students' motivation and engagement and make schools more humane and better places to learn. Meier (1995) reports that close teacher-student relationships allow teachers to demand more of students "without being insensitive or humiliating" (p. 111). Eccles et al. (1993) found that supportive teacher-student relationships are particularly important for low-performing students. Wehlage et al. (1989) found that in schools that functioned as communities of support, teachers' relationships with students could be a source of social capital. Teachers, Wehlage et al. explain, could help students at risk of dropping out to recover themselves and "rebuild the social bonds that tie students to adults and the norms of the school" (p. 25). In other words, relationships are a source of potential newfound school success. Newmann & Associates (1996) report that adult relationships also benefit schools and student achievement. They claim that schools characterized by a strong professional community in which adults have cooperative and collaborative relationships, focused on instruction, benefit student performance.

In schools that are communities of commitment, caring relationships, rather than regulations, are the organizational building blocks, the pathways for communicating and enacting commitments; that is, beliefs, values, goals, and promises. Because commitment inheres in caring relationships—indeed, caring relationships are often considered a condition for commitment—they are central to the operation of schools. What do powerful, caring student-teacher and professional relationships look like in schools that are communities of commitment? What characterizes them? How do they work? How do schools make them happen and support them? How are they used to leverage student achievement? How do they influence values that inform how teachers define their role? How are they a source for collective action that can benefit the goals and commitments of individuals and the school community, or how do they nurture and how are they a source of social capital? The exploration of these questions is the focus of this chapter. A snapshot of relationships at work at Hodgson Vocational Technical High School begins our exploration.

A SNAPSHOT OF A POWERFUL RELATIONSHIP

Standing in front of an audience of 25 family members, friends, and teachers, the high school principal and district superintendent, and a national network TV reporter, Stanley, Hodgson baseball team's stocky, 18-year-old star batter and catcher began to weep. Dressed in a Victorian morning suit, striped tie, high hat, spats, and patent leather shoes, Stanley, along with two peers, had just successfully completed a 1 ½-hour oral presentation and defense on the architecture and construction of a 3/4-scale model Edwardian, shingle-style house that his team had constructed. Not only had the team designed and executed the construction of the model; they had researched it, written reports on it, and responded to questions from a committee of teachers who sought evidence of the depth of their knowledge and understanding on the architecture and construction of Edwardian shingle-style houses.

Struggling to compose himself, Stanley searched his pockets for a handkerchief, dabbed his cheeks dry, made several unsuccessful attempts to lift his head and clear his throat, and then in a breaking voice described to his audience the journey that took him to this celebratory day. Injured earlier in the year and left unable to play for most of the championship season, Stanley, who was never an ambitious student, had sunk into silence and depression. He explained:

> When I came back from the hospital, I was having a lot of
> trouble with my project. I was having a lot of trouble with
> everything. I was having a lot of trouble mentally with differ-
> ent things going through my head. I had thoughts I couldn't
> tell no one. Very terrible, terrible thoughts.

Again, as emotion overcame him, his broad chest heaved and tears streamed down his face. Taking a deep breath, he paused and tried to collect himself. Struggling to keep his chin up and his eyes dry, he mumbled, "Terrible. Couldn't tell no one. Terrible."

Warm rays of sun bounced off the backs of white metal chairs, neatly arranged in three rows on a broad stretch of freshly cut, spring-green grass just outside Hodgson's carpentry shop. Here Stanley's audience sat anxiously transfixed on this May afternoon. Looking directly at Special Education English teacher Carolyn Steinwedel and Carpentry Shop teacher Dave Lutz, both evaluators of his project, Stanley said, "Without these two people, I wouldn't be standing here." Some of those listening later whispered about the comment's ominous innuendo. After handing flowers first to Steinwedel and then Lutz, along with gifts students traditionally give to their teachers after such presentations, Stanley hugged each of them tightly and lingered in their embraces. Steinwedel sobbed and was soon joined by another tearful colleague, Darnell Grandell, chair of the Mathematics Department and also Stanley's teacher.

Earlier, Lutz and Steinwedel had confided their struggle, frustration, and perseverance in getting Stanley through the school's Senior

Project. At no point until the presentation was completed were Lutz and Steinwedel sure that Stanley would transcend his depression and resistance to complete the project. Lutz explained:

> Stanley has not pulled his weight throughout this. He [has] just now at exhibition time decided to take this seriously and he's frustrated. When he busted his arm, he felt sorry for himself. He stopped working. On everything! I had in-your-face confrontations with him. I told him he had to stop feeling sorry for himself and do the project. It went on and on like this!

At the final rehearsal only a couple of hours before the presentation, Lutz instructed the three boys to practice, but Stanley was missing his index cards with the prompts for his part. They were with his friend who had left the school to buy the flowers Stanley would present to his teachers. Nonetheless, an exasperated Lutz insisted they practice their presentation. The boys proceeded with their rehearsal, which was punctuated with tension as Stanley forgot the sequence of his parts and threw off his partners, requiring them all to regroup regularly. From time to time, the boys glanced beseechingly at Lutz who stood steadfast, his arms folded across his chest, and relentlessly demanded that they complete their rehearsal. After several adjustments, but none too happily, they did.

Steinwedel explained that Stanley was so late submitting the research paper required for the Senior Project, that his English teacher refused to even consider accepting it, which meant he would automatically receive a failing grade. Despite Steinwedel's efforts at negotiation, Stanley's English teacher contended that to accept his paper at such a late date after she had supported him through several extensions would violate her standards and be unfair to other students. Unless he completed the research report, he would not be allowed to work on the Edwardian house or perform the oral presentation. Completing the house and presenting it publicly were important to him. And, if he received high enough grades on the construction of the house and on the oral presentation, which required him to synthesize learnings from his research and construction, he could still pass the project. Nonetheless, it was a risk. He would have to complete the research paper knowing that a failing grade was a foregone conclusion, and even if he could get beyond his resentment about the automatic failure, Stanley was not confident that he had the capacity to complete it. He might put in the effort and get no return.

Stanley was dejected. Steinwedel decided to guide (read push) him through the completion of the research paper. And with her support, he completed it. Helped by the coordinated efforts of Lutz, Steinwedel, and a third teacher, all of whom comprised the committee charged to guide him through the Senior Project, Stanley passed.

THE NATURE OF CARING RELATIONSHIPS IN A SCHOOL SETTING

Stanley's story illuminates the nature of student-teacher relationships in schools that are communities of commitment. These relationships are characterized by strong, caring ties that are analogous to family bonds. Stanley's situation shows how these close, family-like bonds can be transformative. That is, they can play a critical role in changing individuals' possibilities, as they did in Stanley's case, where what could have easily been a failure became a success. These relationships can be transcendent, and in being transcendent they can leverage social and personal development and academic achievement, as occurred in Stanley's case. Stanley's relationships with Lutz and Steinwedel helped him assert personal discipline to transcend himself and a troubling time in his life that otherwise might have resulted in school and perhaps personal failure. Through these relationships Stanley was able to complete a significant task—the Senior Project. He was also able to achieve personal and school community goals—his desire to complete the construction of the Edwardian house and his school's desire to successfully academically challenge vocational education students.

Students-and-faculty relationships at the Urban Academy and International High School also demonstrate caring and family-like bonds that have the power to leverage student achievement. Indeed, Urban Academy students' comments suggest that caring relationships may be the single most powerful variable in turning around those who have not succeeded. "Caring," explained one student, "is the main thing. You can't get educational until you get personal."

Another commented, "It changes things a lot when teachers care about you."

Another remarked, "Caring is what makes us want to go to school every day."

At UA, remarked teacher Nancy Jachim, "Every kid is grabbed by some adult. No one is unconnected." UA codirector Herb Mack pointed out that the school's small size of 120 enables students to make their own attachments to adults. On occasions when students and faculty have not made attachments on their own, Mack, whom students regard as a surrogate father, reaches out personally to help them connect or at staff meetings seeks out those faculty members who think they have a rapport with the students in question.

When students are without a family, UA faculty members have become their advocates and negotiated social services as needed. They have secured homes for students who have had none, medical care for students who are ill, and financial aid for students who have had none. They intervene when students who live in group homes have problems. They assist with bail arrangements when students get into trouble with the law.

Like family members, they keep tabs on graduates who have no family. They see them on holidays. If they are away at a college, they phone them. UA codirector Ann Cook regularly sends them care packages of food. She and others negotiate with their college financial aid officers to secure adequate financial aid packages. Troy, a graduate whose mother died while he was enrolled at UA, regularly returns to tell his former teachers how he is doing. During one visit, he explained, "UA is as close and important as my regular family. [UA teachers] inspired me to do a lot."

Cook, Social Studies teacher Avram Barlowe, and Math teacher Wally Warshawsky commented that they and their colleagues take on the role of surrogate family because no one else is available to take care of the students and they refuse not to respond to their circumstances. As Warshawsky sees it, the faculty's role as surrogate family serves the school's educational commitments:

> A lot of kids have a lot of problems and you help them fix
> their problems, but in some cases you have to fix it for them
> because it's out of their hands. Such as when a kid who has
> no place to live—you can't just do nothing about it. You have
> to try to figure out a place so that the kid can be someplace
> so that they can function. If they have specific medical prob-
> lems, you have to be able to do something about it. They
> may not be able to, whereas we know better because we're
> adults, and we know the ropes of how to get stuff done, and

we have connections that they don't have. So there are those kinds of areas. You have to look at it from the point of view of how we can make them take more control of their lives in the academic area which is what we're supposed to be doing, mainly; but not just that because sometimes if they can't take some control of their lives in the nonacademic areas, it's going to affect the academic area also.

At International High School caring relationships help students transcend the isolation of language barriers, the loneliness of family separations, and the fears of being in a strange culture. Students described their relationships with teachers in terms of family. Teachers are "second parents" or "older friends" to whom they can turn when they need help. Many make reference to their teachers' concern for their physical and emotional well-being. One student commented, "I will not forget the teachers help me in my need."

International's principal, Eric Nadelstern, explained that "Every kid connects to at least one adult." Approximately one third of International's faculty members, explained Nadelstern, volunteer to become surrogate family to students who are separated from their biological families. On major holidays, these teachers have taken students to their homes to make sure they have a sense of family. Elio, a graduate of International, recalled an episode when Nadelstern had acted as his surrogate parent. Elio's parents, having remained in their native country, were not available for his report card conferences with his teachers; nor were other relatives. When Nadelstern discovered Elio alone on Parent-Teacher Conference Day, he went to each class with Elio, introducing himself as his guardian and discussing all of his grades with the teachers.

Across the schools intimate, trusting relationships and teacher persistence in response to student resistance are powerful levers for students' social and personal development and academic achievement. I now discuss the nature and operation of relationships in schools that are communities of commitment.

Intimacy

By intimacy, I mean that teachers know students well. They know them as individuals. They know what is happening in their lives, socially and at home. They know students as learners in their class and in the classes of their colleagues. Charles, a Hodgson plumbing student, remarked: "All the teachers know me in the school. Mr. Allen knows where I live, how I live, what's my last name, what's my middle name, how old I am, my telephone number. He knows everything about me."

Being known as an individual and as a student, being named, and being acknowledged are very important to students. One Urban Academy student said, "Everybody knows your name. They say hello to you. You interact with people."

Another stated, "Here [at UA] you're a person. You're somebody here."

Another commented, "There's more personalized attention here—teachers know you and you know them."

Another explained, "[Teachers] take a personal interest in you. That makes school a whole different experience."

As this student's remark reveals, being known, naming names, strengthens the connections among individuals and with the school as a community: "If something happens here, everyone talks about it; they mention names."

Across the schools, being known creates a safety net that makes it difficult for students to fall through the cracks. The safety net is at work in Stanley's relationships as Lutz and Steinwedel use their knowledge of Stanley's personal circumstances and his needs as a learner to support him to perform and to direct their actions.

An Urban Academy student explained, "If you're not here you're missed. Your home is called."

Another commented, "They do what they have to do to keep kids in school. If I need to get up early, they'll call me."

Another explained, "At UA they try to help you. Talk to you. Try to see what you're good at. They work with your weak points."

At Hodgson, Kathy, a dental lab student, said:

Teachers are more one-on-one with the kids. At other schools the [assistant] principals just know you if you get into trouble. In Hodgson [assistant] principals come up to you and ask you how you're doing and all. [They] know the kids more.

International High School Math and Science teacher Simon Cohen asserts that teachers' opportunities to know students well is their primary and most effective strategy for supporting and monitoring students: "The most effective thing is basically every teacher knows every student, basically knows where every student belongs all the time, has a relationship with each student." He contends that teachers use their knowledge of students to leverage achievement.

Teachers' knowledge of students enables them to develop effective instructional interventions. At Hodgson, one student explained, "When I needed help the teachers knew because I wasn't trying. They would sit there and talk to me." Teachers could apply an intervention that was likely to succeed because they had the knowledge to accurately interpret this student's behavior.

Several International students mentioned that teachers know just when they will need extra learning support, because at those times teachers rewrite text material in "simple English," make photocopies of materials from their own personal books, and give them examples to increase their understanding. Several students imagined teachers spending "nights and days doing work for them," especially on text revisions. Teachers were not, as one student asserted, merely teaching "from the book, which we can't understand that much of."

Hodgson Math teacher Robert Rhies described how conversations and personal interactions with students over time led him to change both his math curriculum and teaching practice from the lecture/ memorizing algorithms method to a problem-solving, activity-based method designed to help students understand the theories behind the algorithms:

> I asked my [Math] students, "When did you stop liking school?"
> They kept saying, "When teachers began to lecture." I had the desire to make the [math] material more interesting for the kids. . . . I wanted to increase students' interest in math because if they are more interested, they will pursue math after school.

Opportunities for teachers to know students well can also evoke a deep understanding and acceptance of students as adolescents, as it does in Lutz and Steinwedel's responses to Stanley. They treat his behavior as an opportunity to help him mature by structuring occasions for him to take responsibility rather than as reasons to punish him for his irre-

sponsibility and resistance. Lutz insists that Stanley rehearse for his presentation, even without his cue cards, and Steinwedel insists that he complete his research paper even though it cannot achieve a passing grade.
The relationship makes them more than content instructors; it makes
them adults helping youngsters learn and practice habits necessary for
successful adulthood in their community.

Opportunities for knowing students well also strengthen teachers'
attachments and commitment to students, as Hodgson's Dale
Derrickson, who teaches machine maintenance technology (repair and
maintenance of machines, mechanical equipment, and plumbing, electrical, heating, and air-conditioning systems), explains:

> We get to spend a lot of time with [our students] and really
> get to know them. It really helps a lot. . . . We see a lot of
> personal growth. . . . We get to know them so well; we don't
> have that indifference. Once you get to know the students
> you care about them more.

Trust

At the foundation of relationships between teachers and students is
trust. As students explain, trust means that teachers can be counted on
to be accessible, accepting, and helpful with students' personal, social,
and educational needs. One student at UA explained, "There is always
a teacher to help you with your problems, whether they are academic or
personal."

Another said, "I know if I need someone, there will be someone
there for me."

Another remarked, "I'm sure every teacher in this school has had
some kid go to them, like cry their eyes out, whether it be about school
or anything else."

At International, Ana, a Peruvian tenth grader, remarked: "You
can trust people."

Christina, a Polish student, agreed: "We can trust the teachers. Is
comfortable to talk to them." She explained that when students are ill,
teachers inquire after them.

Other students mentioned how teachers encouraged them to
express their anxieties and concerns. Typical is Vietnamese student
Pham Nam's comment, which reveals his faith in teachers to help him:

"Like, 'You scared?' They'll ask you, 'Tell us what happened. Someone bother you? You fail the test?' So they can solve the problem. They gonna give you the good advice."

When Hodgson students need help, they go to their empathetic teachers and administrators. Charles remarked:

[We] got [assistant] principals and teachers here that we can talk to. They can understand us and put things together. They can adjust themselves in our shoes and know how we feel about the situation and whether they can do something about it. We have communication here.

Mary, a cosmetology student, explained that "Teachers say, 'If you have a problem, come to me when you want to.'"

Richard, a Hodgson Visual Communication Arts major, explained:

Ms. Piretti [Visual Communications Shop teacher], you can talk to her and she'll find something for you. She'll make sure you know what's going on and which direction you're going in. You don't even need guidance counselors if you ask me.

Earl, a Culinary Arts student, commented: "If you're a failure, you know that they have people to help you. For example, when I speak to Mr. Grandell [Math teacher], he sits down and explains it until you know what you are doing."

Travis (a Cosmetology major) said:

Talking to my teachers really helped me. All of the teachers have helped me. None of the teachers here let me down. They got me to play football and I played for four years. Now I'm gonna go to college. I got a little scholarship.

Students can count on their teachers because the schools give the teachers the authority and autonomy to be accountable. The schools deem their teachers trustworthy. Teachers can and do make decisions based on their professional judgment as it maps against the mission and values of the school and the goals of the students. Students assert that teachers can be trusted because they make sufficient time for access to them. Students measure teachers' commitment by the time teachers devote to them. Typical are comments such as this one by Mary: "For the most part, teachers give up their time to help you out."

Similarly, Kelly, a Culinary student, said, "What helps is that teachers give you their time. They're willing to stay after school and lunch period."

Steinwedel explained that teachers intentionally communicate their accessibility to students:

> We present ourselves in such a way to let the students know we're very open to what they have to do. I think they know that they can come in here and shut the door and scream every now and then and we're not going to hold it against them.

Hodgson's principal Steve Godowsky is not only accessible to students; he makes them his top priority.

At the Urban Academy students trust teachers to accept with good humor their adolescent contradictions manifest in their sometimes regressive and dependent behavior, which is publicly displayed in their sometimes satirical cartoons and caricatures of staff members that capture the essence of their appearance and teaching style, but primarily in 10 years of cajoling, demanding, pleading, rebuking, and humorous notes to codirector Mack, all of which paper the 25-by-15-foot wall adjacent to his desk. Typical are these:

> Dear Herb, I hate you. Love, _____.

> Dear Herb, I would just like to let you know that I *would* have handed in my "Issues" paper, if I could. You see, as I was attempting to pick it up this morning, it jumped off my desk and bit my toe. Then it hid under my bed. Once I catch it, I'll bring it in. I would just like to let you know that I have to lure it out with lots of white-out and a pen, which in my room are hard to find.

> We need paper towels in the girls' bathroom, Herb. Get them!

> Herb Law: Thou shalt not be late; Thou shalt always do your work . . . .

> Don't ask "why" unless you have 45 minutes.

Hey Herb, i'll [sic] pay you a quarter if you finish grading my *late* paper. (Posthaste). I need to go to college!!!

Herb, My first Note to you! It's a *complaint!* Ha thought you get off easy, Huh!! I like the fish candies, so fillem up! Now!

Herb—call my dad! Before I kill him!

This sampling of notes indicates the degree of affection, attachment, and trust students have for their principal, enough to make demands on him, to have expectations of him to be responsive in all areas of their lives, and to make these expectations public and in a petulant and familiar tone that transgresses the conventional boundaries of authority that typically define student-teacher and student-principal relationships. The school's public display of these symbols of faculty-student relationships signifies the staff commitment to and trust in the students and their school.

Student Resistance and Teacher Persistence

As in Stanley's relationship with Lutz and Steinwedel, teacher persistence in response to student resistance is common in the relationships between teachers and students at the Urban Academy and International High School. Across schools, student resistance manifests itself in multiple forums: students find ways to avoid challenging educational tasks, habits of work, and social obligations. Stanley "forgets" his cue cards for the rehearsal of his presentation, he is late in completing his English research paper despite several extensions, and his negative attitude and continuously disappointing behavior frustrate his peers and teachers. Godowsky and several Hodgson teachers report that the majority of Hodgson students choose the school thinking that they can avoid academics. One Social Studies teacher explained:

> When I informed my ninth graders the third week of
> September that we had a heavy-duty writing program and
> that's what they were sticking to, they told me flat out that
> they came here so they wouldn't have to do academic work.

At International, students were in the habit of making private bargains with themselves to get low grades or incompletes in some courses, usually those more challenging, while devoting greater effort to courses where they felt more confident. Many resist using English, preferring to communicate in their native language. They express ambivalence about the interdependence and social responsibility required for collaborative group work, the pedagogy at the core of International's instructional program.

At the Urban Academy, especially where students have had numerous unsuccessful school experiences, many have a long history of resistance. Almost all have difficulty submitting work on time. Many have never read a book to completion. Most are used to making very little investment in their schoolwork and are satisfied with perfunctory efforts. Their time management, organization, and work-study skills are poor.

Despite this, in each of the schools, teachers meet students' resistance by persisting in their demands for quality performance, coupling them with the support students need to attain it. Teachers' unrelenting persistence is evidence of their commitment to their students and to their school's educational mission. Many students describe teachers' persistence as "push." Typical are these comments by Hodgson students:

> [Teachers] push you. If you start drifting, they'll get right on
> your case. They'll push you, push you, and push you until
> you get up. I wasn't too good in any of my subjects and then
> when I came to this school, as soon as I sat down in class,
> they said, "Well, we're gonna expect a lot from you in this
> class." And from there on, they just push you and push you.

Another remarked: "[The teachers] really expect a lot from you. . . . and they have people to help you."

The process of teachers and students developing bonds and connecting and establishing common ground is itself a lever for improving learning and achievement, as one student notes:

> When I first came here [as a ninth grader], I didn't care
> about nothing. I learned about communication. Once you sit
> down and talk to one of these teachers about how they feel,
> how they want you to do, [you] can turn out as a straight A
> student. They'll tell you that they've been there before and
> they know that you're human, too. They want some A's, too.
> They know where we're coming from when we say that we

can't do a certain problem because they've been there
before themselves. And since they made it, they're gonna
make it sure enough so that we can make it, too.

Often students tearfully explain that they "would not have made it"
without particular teachers, that their teachers never gave up on them,
and that they never believed in themselves until they saw the persistence
of their teachers' belief in them. Teacher persistence, as a Hodgson special education student suggests, can be particularly significant where students are fragile:

Without Mr. Coleman [a Special Education assistant] I would
not have passed because I kept on saying, "I'm gonna give
up. I'm gonna give up." But I didn't. And then I did my
presentation and I got a 92. I would never think I could do
that because I kept saying, "I'm not gonna do it."
I was gonna quit school. I was supposed to graduate
last year. But with Mr. Coleman's "Julia, you can do it," I
stayed in school. . . . [Mr. Coleman] came to my shop and
asked if I needed help. He was on my committee. I could go
to him any time I needed.

Recalling Stanley's story, his teachers persist in their demands and
support for his performance by not letting him fall through the cracks by
dropping out. They increase their attention. They sustain their high
expectations for his performance by creating opportunities and structures that deliberately push him through obstacles until he completes the
requisite tasks, and they use their relationship as needed. Lutz is in
Stanley's face. He insists on rehearsal even though Stanley is unpre-
pared, even though Stanley has habitually fallen short. Steinwedel advocates on Stanley's behalf and then devotes the time and attention he
needs to complete his English research paper.
Over and over, Stanley's teachers make the option of disengagement and failure difficult for him to choose. Instead he is confronted by
demands for responsiveness and responsibility by teachers who are
responsive to his needs and who take responsibility for helping him
through his task. Teachers' use of committed and trusting relationships
and their persistence despite Stanley's resistance mitigates the educational risks inherent in the tasks Stanley needs to complete and keep him

from totally abandoning them. The teachers make it harder to fail than
succeed.

Similarities abound at the Urban Academy. "Human Sexuality"
teacher Gail Lemelbaum describes the nature of teacher persistence
there:

> It's the punch and stroke method. We have nudge and nag
> and punch and stroke: "You better get that homework done.
> I'm really sick of this. What is this! You can do this!" Then,
> "I really miss it when you don't turn your work in." It's
> demanding a lot and at the same time being very under-
> standing.

Students' stories of their relationships with teachers reveal
the "nudge and nag and punch and stroke" nature of teacher persistence, students' resistance, their capitulation to teacher demands, and
their understanding of teachers' commitment to their achievement.
Whitney, who was a chronic cutter in her former elite NYC high school,
explains:

> [Teachers] want you to do your work; so if you have prob-
> lems, they'll be like, "Well, I really want you to get this
> done." And if they see you need a little more motivation,
> they'll say, "Come, sit down."
>   You're like, "No. I gotta go."
>   "Hey, sit down. You have to get this done. This is what
> you have to do." They'll sit down and talk with you. Make
> sure you get it in your head.
>   You can't get out of it because I have not once gotten
> out of having to do anything. Never. The teachers will try to
> help you do better. They will try to bring your standard up.
> You can try for as high as you can go.

Kathleen, who had attended parochial schools prior to enrolling at
UA, stated: "If you have a problem, if you need tutoring, or if you need
some extra help with something, [teachers] will be on your back all the
time until you sit down with them and actually talk. You know they'll be
there."

Mary-Grace, who enrolled at UA after having been expelled from
Catholic school because she refused to remove pierced ornaments

from her tongue, eyebrow, chin, and nose, described how teachers "nudge":

> [The teachers] sit down with you and help you, like, "What's the problem? What don't you understand? Let me help you. Let me rephrase it. Let me talk to you in a different way." You know, anything that can help you get into this work and help you understand it in a different way.

Although UA effectively pushes students to increase their productivity, teachers need to be sensitive to the fragility of their achievements. English teacher Rachel Wyatt explains:

> [Teachers will say] "Can we be flexible at this end to create some way for you to get it done?" So the kid's always an active partner in these things, but you can still feel minute-to-minute frustration.

Successfully pushing students, Lemelbaum points out, can present teachers and schools with an enduring dilemma, redolent of that confronted by Stanley's English teacher: "How do we hold kids responsible for meeting standards and wanting to provide them with unlimited opportunities?" As teachers' experiences in the three schools reveal, a blanket policy is not an adequate response to this dilemma. Faculty need to have the authority to make decisions on the merits of the individual situation so that decisions are guided by individual students' learning needs for the present as well as for their future and the school's needs to sustain its credibility as an effective learning community. Where there is strong commitment to both students and the school community, faculty can be trusted to make balanced decisions in the interests of both the individual and the community as they do in the International team meeting and on Stanley's Senior Project.

At International, teacher persistence has led to and been supported by organizational changes generated by the faculty. Teachers' commitment to increasing students' performance levels and reducing opportunities for them to compromise their performance in particular courses contributed to the faculty's decision to restructure the school into self-contained, interdisciplinary clusters of 100 students and 5 or 6 teachers, whereby teachers could know a cohort well and work together closely to monitor and support them. The self-contained cluster structure enables

cluster teachers to meet together with students about whose performance they are concerned and collaboratively problem-solve. Meetings
between an individual student and all of his or her teachers can be very
powerful. Together teachers and the student confront patterns of behavior and performance that are unproductive and problematic and
construct a strategy for improvement that builds on the strengths of
teachers and the student. As clusters behave like a small community,
converging on the issues of particular students, falling through the cracks
becomes more difficult for students. School data revealed that immediately after the implementation of this cluster organization,
International's course pass rate increased by 5%.

In response to students' ambivalence about collaborative group
work, International's teachers take the time to explain the reasoning
undergirding the school's commitment to it. Teachers hope that their
explanations will increase students' understanding, engagement, and
cooperation with their demands and diminish their anxieties. When
some students in Dina Heisler's Humanities class objected to collaborative work groups, she discussed her and the school's rationale with individual and small groups of students:

> They asked, "Why is it important to learn their work in a
> group?" [I discussed with them] the fact that for the rest
> of their lives they're going to be in one kind of group or
> another. Collaborative learning provides students with
> opportunities to learn how to resolve interpersonal conflicts
> in the context of a team, what it means to honor a contract,
> and what the dilemmas of leadership are.

Students' comments suggest that teachers' responsiveness and
respect expand their capacity for tolerating their ambivalence and the
trade-offs and ambiguities inherent in collaboration and finding ways to
be productive individually and as members of a group. One student stated, "The best and the worst moments were working in groups."

Another explained,

> When the people are placed in groups, they would work as
> hard as they can in order to get a good grade so that they
> should care not only for themselves, but as well as the others
> and do well. That's when everything would work out, but
> sometimes it depends on the people.

Another said:

> I always found out that some people know something that I
> don't know, and I can tell them what they can't do. We learn
> from each other. There is nobody who knows everything
> best [sic] than somebody else. Once people feel important,
> that they could be helpers, then they open up and talk. First
> they are very scared.

Another remarked:

> Sometimes, I don't really like [the groups] because not
> everyone's equal, not everyone knows as much. Sometimes
> the people who know more have to put the project together
> and the rest of the people don't do it as well. And the peo-
> ple, they're not so happy about it. That's one thing that I
> don't like about the groups.

Steve Lindberg, Social Studies and Math teacher, believes that students' resistance occurs because they don't have the knowledge and
skills necessary to collaborate effectively and because their prior learning environments devalued collaborative behavior. Therefore, asserts
Lindberg, it becomes the school's responsibility to teach those skills necessary for effective collaboration. The opportunity for teachers and students to have close relationships facilitates ongoing, respectful communication where both can be responsive to the concerns of each other and
where teachers can adjust their pedagogy to respond to students' anxieties without compromising the pedagogical principles of their school.

Teacher persistence in response to student resistance is so pervasive in the three schools that they could each be said to have a culture
of teacher persistence. What I mean by a culture of teacher persistence
is that persistence as a teacher response to student resistance to educational challenge is not isolated, idiosyncratic, or serendipitous, in which
case it would be available only to those students lucky enough to be in
the classes of particular teachers. Rather, teacher persistence in response
to student resistance is a norm of professional practice; it is an expectation for all teachers and is evoked not necessarily by the personal ethos
of individual teachers, but by the mission and value system of the
schools, which in this instance envision themselves as caring learning
communities committed to developing students intellectually and

preparing them for their future either in the workplace or at postsecondary institutions. This vision and commitment set a context for schoolwide expectations for teacher roles and behavior, which in these cases means that teachers hold themselves accountable for eliciting student learning and achievement. Since that requires persistence, they hold themselves, individually and collectively, accountable for persistence. International High School Social Studies teacher Aaron Listhaus expresses this ethos:

> We view a student's failure as our own failure, recognizing that there are some problems we can't solve. But generally we need to support all of our students so that they do pass and move on. . . . Whatever we think is going to work is what we'll do.

The value that each school's culture places on teacher persistence is evident in the status that individual acts of persistence convey upon teachers and by rituals that celebrate persistence. While teachers do not walk around announcing or asserting their persistence, they invariably regale or one-up each other (or any willing listener) with commentary on or tales of student resistance countered by their "heroic" efforts of persistence and perseverance and ultimately conquest as resistance surrenders and triumphant students accept challenging projects. The story of Stanley is typical. But so is this gleefully related comment of Dental Lab teacher Al Angel: "We drag students through the Senior Project kicking and screaming!"

There is this Senior Project tale told by Hodgson English chair MaryAn Scarbrough:

> [The student] and I and the shop teacher sat down and I said, "Okay, now you tell him—the shop teacher—what you're going to do for your product in shop. What are you going to make?" Because we had talked about what he was going to research.
>
>   And he said, "This is what I want to do."
>   And the shop teacher said, "Too easy."
>   And the kid said, "Well, okay, *this* is what I'll do."
>   And the shop teacher said, "Nope. Too easy."
>   So the kid said, "What would you like me to do?"
>   The shop teacher said, "This is what I'd like you to do."
>   And the kid said, "Well, that's hard."

> And both the shop teacher and I said, "Yes. But it's doable,
> isn't it?"
> The kid said, "Yeah. I could do it if I really put my mind to it."
> That's what we want. (Ancess & Darling-Hammond, 1994,
> p. 9)

Teaching in these instances includes expanding students' learning ambitions.

Embedded in the culture of teacher persistence is the normalization of student resistance. When the faculty can regard student resistance as normative rather than as pathological or as willful disobedience or a deeply rooted character flaw, it becomes just one of the variables in the school constellation that factors into how education is organized and delivered for high levels of achievement. Resistance is understood in an educational context and planned for. At the Urban Academy, Social Studies teacher Avram Barlowe explains that teachers understand and accept the fact that if they persist in their demands for students to meet personal and academic challenges, they also have to "tolerate their regressions."

UA's Nancy Jachim contends that if schools expect students to embrace their priorities, they need to embrace their students' priorities and to be responsive to their developmental needs:

> The school's priority is academic; the students' is usually
> social and emotional. Kids want to be loved, thought of as
> beautiful–their agenda is to be cared for. Teachers want them
> to learn academics.

To International's Charlie Glassman, who has argued that the school's job is to support students to mature, immaturity is normative.

One Hodgson Social Studies teacher says: "Many of our students are very undermotivated to achieve academically. They really don't care and so they sell themselves short."

Maintenance Technology teacher Dale Derrickson agrees and explains how teachers adapt their teaching so students can transcend their resistance:

> I think some of these students are just turned off to school.
> They haven't felt interested or successful. A lot are very

intelligent kids. It's just that the way they've been taught in
the past is not the way they learn. A lot of these kids don't
see in the abstract. They're learners that actually want to
apply what they're doing. Give them something concrete,
then it starts to make a lot more sense to them.

These are not criticisms of students or characterizations of defi-
ciencies. Rather, they are statements of fact, descriptions of how students
are, information that is useful for teaching and learning. These publicly
acknowledged understandings and perspectives of student resistance
strengthen teachers' commitment and the school's commitment to persist in the face of resistance in no small part because these ways of understanding, of interpreting students' behavior, protect teachers, individually and collectively, from feeling rejected, fatigued, and defeated.
Because these ways of understanding student behavior are embedded in
and emerge from the school culture, the school as a community and the
school's commitments to its vision and its students are also protected
from the assault that student resistance can be and the negative culture
of failure and blame that often results.

LEVERAGING RELATIONSHIPS FOR SOCIAL DEVELOPMENT
AND ACADEMIC ACHIEVEMENT

In each of the schools there are norms of practice for using relationships
to leverage students' social development and intellectual achievement.
Relationships are not used for the purposes of hanging out, paling
around, or excusing poor performance. Rather, relationships are a pedagogical tool that enables teachers to care not only about their students
but also about their students' learning. This use of relationships requires
diffuse roles for teachers. Teachers at Hodgson, International, and the
Urban Academy take on a variety of roles, functioning as instructors,
advisors, confidantes, advocates, tutors, facilitators, mediators, and surrogate family. Such diffuse roles provide teachers with multiple opportunities and entry points to establish close, caring, and trusting relationships that enable them to know students well—both as students and as
people—from diverse perspectives, and use that knowledge and their
relationship to provide students with personal attention and influence
their behavior.

Undergirding the schools' expectations for teachers to adopt diffuse roles is the assumption that teachers individually and collectively, and teachers' professional judgment, are trustworthy. These are not schools designed to be teacher proof. Rather, these schools depend on teachers. Teachers are not saddled with regulations or narrow and rigidly defined role descriptions that obstruct and conflict with their professional judgment and the interventions they may deem appropriate. Furthermore, teachers' collaborative work structure provides safeguards for their judgments. Teachers work with a set of trusted colleagues in a community of practice, in which they receive feedback on their judgments. As in Stanley's case, when school policies are learner-centered and flexible, and acknowledge the complexities of the learning context, there is room for teachers to respect one another's differences in judgment without feeling that they are betraying students' best interests or their own or the school's standards of practice. Both Stanley's English teacher and Steinwedel can feel confident in the appropriateness of their different judgments regarding his predicament without sacrifice to him.

Relationships also serve the important function of helping teachers to obtain access to students. Access unlocks information that enables teachers to help students in both the personal and academic spheres and to push students beyond self-imposed limits to leverage progress and achievement.

In order to support the use of relationships as levers for student development and achievement, schools need to be organized to function as communities driven by a set of commitments to particular goals and values, where there is time and there are structures for individuals to make attachments. This means that teachers and students must be able to have easy, regular, planned, and unplanned access to one another. Such access keeps teachers up to date on students and makes possible as well as encourages "just-in-time" interventions. Such access facilitates the function of relationships as an important tool to negotiate Lemelbaum's enduring dilemma: "how to hold kids responsible for meeting standards and wanting to provide them with unlimited opportunities."

This dilemma finds resolution in Steinwedel's strategy for Stanley to complete his Senior Project research paper when he can no longer receive credit for it. She is able to use her relationship with him to negotiate its completion because Hodgson's grading policy permits students to pass the Senior Project even if their research paper has received a failing grade—so long as they have completed the research paper. This policy creates openings for interventions, such as relationships, that can mediate students' performance.

All three schools provide multiple opportunities in their structures, schedules, curriculum, instruction, and assessment for formal and informal interactions between students and teachers and for regular and easy access. At International and Hodgson, interdisciplinary teaching and learning clusters, in which a constant group of teachers shares a constant group of students in contiguous classrooms, assure frequent and easy access and formal and informal and planned and unplanned interactions between staff and students. The proximity of students and cluster teachers and the flow of cluster teachers in and out of each other's rooms increase the possibilities for engagement. Teachers assert that this structure encourages them to follow up on students. Performance assessments at each of the schools bring students and teachers together to plan and execute projects and oral presentations by which their achievement in different disciplines and their readiness for graduation is judged.

Each of the schools acknowledges the importance of chemistry in the formation of personal attachment. At the smaller International and UA, teachers and students can either make their own attachments or principals can facilitate them. At the larger Hodgson, students select the teachers for their Senior Project committees and orchestrate their use with as much ease as their committee members oversee their progress. According to faculty and students, this process of self-selecting relationships encourages frequent and informal interaction, increasing opportunities for teacher responsiveness and timely and effective interventions that impact student performance.

Supporting relationships in each school are advisories or advisory-like mechanisms that link a small group of students with a single faculty member whose role it is to know the students well personally and to know their overall progress. Teacher advisors follow up on assignments required for students' courses, help them organize their work and meet deadlines, provide tutoring, and comfort them. They are the primary link to students' other teachers and reinforce their demands. Advisories also provide a forum for students to be visible, assert their voice, and be heard. Some advisories pair students with teachers to whom they already have close attachments—coaches and sports team members, for instance—so that even relationships that are not inherently academic can nonetheless be harnessed to support academic achievement. Advisories meet regularly, usually once or twice weekly. Some stay together through the students' time at their school. Some are multigrade, with a portion of students graduating out and others entering as they enroll in the school.

Each of the schools also schedules regular time for teaching teams to meet, plan, share information, and strategize to support students. Teachers harvest their relationships with students at meetings with colleagues for the goal of academic progress. Additionally, the structure of instruction reinforces the power of relationships to leverage student progress. The relational interaction required for the Senior Project influences the actions of both Stanley and his teachers. Similarly, the teaching arrangements at International and the Urban Academy, where small groups of teachers share the same set of students, ensure the regular and ongoing contact necessary for strong relationships. As teachers explain, they see students all of the time, working in their own and their colleagues' classes and socializing with their peers.

These organizational arrangements increase the power of relationships to bring coherence to the schools' efforts to be cohesive educational communities that can effectively pursue their goals and promote higher levels of student achievement. They formalize the interpersonal responsibility that inheres in relationships and thereby strengthen the schools' internal, face-to-face accountability.

RELATIONSHIPS AS A SOURCE OF SOCIAL CAPITAL

Because the bureaucratic values of hierarchy and efficiency inform the structure and culture of schools, schools are conventionally organized as though relationships are not only unimportant and irrelevant, but an obstacle to efficient operation. However, as Hodgson, International, and Urban Academy demonstrate, relationships can powerfully affect individual students and their teachers, and as a systemic value and strategy, they can affect the school's collective capacity to influence students' social development and intellectual achievement. Students at the three schools comment on how well their teachers know them and how that knowledge is used to help their educational performance. Teachers' remarks about schoolwide practice, such as Lemelbaum's description of "nudge and nag, punch and stroke" pedagogy, allude to the collective impact of relationships.

The intentional and systemic organization of the school community for the purposes of individuals working solo and collectively to use relationships to produce improvements in student performance makes relationships a powerful source of social capital. Social capital refers to the collective capacity of members of a community to cooperatively produce mutually beneficial outcomes (Coleman, 1988). Social capital inheres in the relationships. Because relationships are the predominant agent for generating social capital, for bonding students to teachers, their school's vision, mission, and belief system, they are a powerful force for schools that aim to be communities of commitment.

Social capital has its roots in economic theory, which asserts that relationships developed in the workplace affect the work and are instruments for economic ends as well as the establishment of trust, expectations, and the development and enforcement of norms (Baker, 1983), which, as Coleman points out, affect productivity (1988). In a sociological context, Coleman identifies three forms of social capital: "(1) obligations and expectations which depend on trustworthiness of the social environment, (2) information flow [and] (3) norms. . . ." (1988, p. 119).

Because relationships can affect the establishment of trust and expectations, the development and enforcement of norms, the work and productivity of teachers and students, and the operation of schools, they can function as a source of social capital. We see that at Hodgson, International, and Urban Academy. Teachers' trustworthiness facilitates students' reliance on them, which contributes to stronger student performance. Close, trusting relationships between teachers and students strengthens students' capacity to tackle their resistance to school expectations. Relationships characterized by the interaction of demands and supports strengthen a sense of mutual obligation between teachers and students. Despite the tensions evoked by teachers' persistent demands, students struggle to meet their school's expectations, and the relationships endure strain without breaking up.

The frequent and mutual access that teachers and students have provides teachers with a powerful and current "information flow" on how students are doing. As International's Cohen points out, teachers' most effective pedagogical tool is the capability of knowing students well. Teachers have up-to-date information on students' responses to their school's demands, with opportunities to be responsive and apply appropriate and timely interventions that support the school's expectations for students' learning and productivity. At International, teachers have ongoing conversations with students in order to support the values and activities of collaboration. They create additional learning experiences to help students meet the expectations for collaborative group work.

At the Urban Academy teachers use their relationships to demand and support resistant students to complete their assignments. At Hodgson, teachers use their relationships to strengthen students' confidence so that they endure the struggle of challenging academic tasks. At all three schools, relationships are integral to the schoolwide productivity norms. Teachers continuously apply interventions to help students surmount obstacles to their performance.

In each of the schools, norms for supporting and promoting student achievement are evident in the characteristics that define teacher-student relationships. Teachers are available. They take students' accounts of their problems seriously. They respond to students' personal and academic problems. They persist in efforts to help students personally and to meet school educational obligations. Students are intentionally connected to school adults with whom they have a rapport. The relationships are used for the achievement of students' expectations and the school's expectations for them. There are also opportunities and support for students to transcend self-imposed personal and educational limits.

Social capital theory applied to schools suggests that relationships can be instruments for the achievement of educational goals, what Coleman (1988) and Wehlage (1993) explain as human capital, the knowledge and skills people derive from formal education that allows them to lead productive and purposeful lives. Indeed, without the social capital, assert Coleman (1988) and Wehlage (1993), children cannot have access to human capital or the knowledge and skills that schools are expected to provide for students' future as productive citizens in society.

These assertions suggest that schools must be able to generate social capital in order to perform their educational mission. The dependency of student learning and achievement on relationships illuminates the connection between human and social capital. Relationships in each of the schools urge and support students emotionally and academically to perform at higher levels. Achievement also relies on relationships as most vividly illustrated in Stanley's story, but also in the testimony of students such as one at the Urban Academy who explains that teachers and schools "have to get personal" before students will "get educational."

Fred Newmann, too, points to the connection between caring and trustworthy relationships between children and adults and students' social and intellectual development: "Emotional bonding to adults in the community who nurture trust, hope, and the self-confidence [are] needed to develop intellectual and social competence" (1993, p. 2). According to Newmann, "social capital is grounded in adults with the commitment, competence, and resources to care for children" (1993, p. 2). These adults, as human resources, can be considered social capital when they "are used to enable individual and collective growth" (Newmann, 1993, p. 2). This dynamic of continuous growth that inheres in relationships strengthens the school as a community of commitment, because the growth itself, which is assessed against the school's educational goals, validates and is a manifestation of the school's commitments.

At Hodgson, International, and Urban Academy adults individually and collectively care for students academically as instructors and personally as surrogate parents. The schools provide the resources for caring relationships and teacher commitment in multiple ways. They enact organizational structures—such as small size—which facilitate attachments, interdisciplinary clusters that increase the opportunities for teachers know students well and to have close relationships, and scheduling and spatial arrangements that enable students and teachers to have easy and unplanned access to one another. They establish mechanisms such as advisories, which formalize the use of relationships. They construct diffuse roles for teachers, which enables them to know students well from different perspectives; and they promote values such as personalization and teacher persistence.

Students' moving testimony across the three schools emphasizes the connection between their individual relationships with school adults and their individual growth. Stanley's powerful confession, that without his teachers—without those committed, enduring persistent relationships—he would not have been celebrating an educational and personal victory, mirrors Coleman's observation that social capital makes "possible the achievement of certain ends that in its absence would not be possible" (1988, p. 98). When relationships are a systemic tool for student achievement, they can be used to powerful and equitable effect, and students need not be victims of the luck of their draw.

CONCLUSION

Individually and collectively, relationships have a powerful impact on a school's capacity to influence students' social and academic development and indeed, their lives. This chapter illuminates the ways in which students' relationships with their teachers are personally important to students, how they impact their performance and development, how teachers use relationships for educational purposes, how schools organize themselves to use relationships as a predominant educational strategy, and how relationships are a resource for student and school community development and performance. The adoption of relationships as a formal educational strategy requires reconceptualizing, reorganizing, and broadening the traditional notions of the high school teachers' role, which is usually limited to that of specialized content disseminator. In order to utilize the potential of relationships as a resource, schools need to reconfigure themselves, no longer as bureaucracies but instead as communities, communities that are defined and driven by educational commitments. Relationships tap into the most compelling human need to be known and to be connected, to have attachments, to be cared for, and to count. By responding to this need in the context of educational goals, schools can honor their commitment to the social and intellectual development of their students and increase students' investment in and commitment to their own education and future.

CHAPTER 4

Teaching and Learning for Making Meaning

"You're not just listening to a teacher lecture you. You're talking to other kids your age."

—a student

Early in her book *The Power of Their Ideas*, Deborah Meier compellingly connects the importance of teaching and learning for making meaning to good citizenship and the vitality of democracy itself:

> Public schools can train us for political conversation across divisions of race, class, religion, and ideology. It is often in the clash of irreconcilable ideas that we can learn how to test or revise ideas or invent new ones. Both teachers and students need to search for metaphors that work across ideological, historical, and personal differences. . . . Differences make things complicated. But dealing with the complicated is what training for good citizenship is all about. Ideas–the ways we organize knowledge–are the medium of exchange in democratic life, just as money is in the marketplace. (1995, pp. 7–8)

Conversations that make public the "ways we organize knowledge," that confront diverse perspectives, that stimulate the examination and reexamination of unexamined and conflicting ideas, that seek common ground–metaphors that transcend differences, that embrace complexity are all acts of meaning making, acts that fulfill the human need to make sense of what we think, feel, and experience, of our world and the worlds of others–past, present, and future.

Teaching and learning for such meaning making present challenges for schools because, as Meier explains, "We're not accustomed to recognizing the power of each other's ideas [and] it's easier to take flight" (1995, p. 10). And in this current compliance-driven, one-size-fits-all standardized test, accountability culture propelled by the marketplace needs where teachers are coerced into transforming curriculum into test-preparation and short-answer knowledge fragments, teaching and learning for making meaning seems to have gotten lost. The dubious assumption that test-driven teaching will improve instructional quality (Grant, 2001) can actually encourage the repression of school- and classroom-specific meaning making instructional efforts. Indeed, with looming threats of firings and school closings, teaching and learning that emphasize making meaning instead of higher test scores can be perilous.

Yet equally perilous is the abandonment of teaching and learning for making meaning. Making meaning is important not only to the future character of our society but also to students' sense of a personal future and a satisfying life–the "good life" promised by our democracy. Especially where students find meaninglessness in their present and confusion or devastation in their personal or historical past, there is little reason to invest in their future or in the present opportunities and pathways to a future. Alienation from active citizenship; and withdrawal from a sense of agency from the possibility of the work for a meaningful life and community, and from the meaning making required for such a life and community become inevitable. Learned helplessness, a sense of powerlessness, cynicism, psychic deracination, and despair become inescapable. As Meier points out, without public and personal meaning making at the core of teaching and learning we place democracy in peril:

> Children grow up, and the habits of mind they bring to both the workplace and the polling place will determine our common fate. It is quite possible that American society can develop a viable economy that ignores the fate of vast numbers of its citizens, one not dependent upon a universally well-educated public. But only at a cost to democracy, itself. . . . (1995, p. 6)

Those habits of mind are also the tools that individuals need to examine and make sense of their lives, their culture, their people, the past, their circumstances, society, and the world. They are the tools students need in order to explore those issues, questions, and dilemmas that confront them; to examine themselves, their worldview and other worldviews; and to find their voices, develop their identities, and strengthen their senses of agency and possibility. In particular, students who have been historically and systematically marginalized, devalued, and underserved because of their ethnic or racial background, social and socio-economic status, or learning style need an education that helps them sort out the myths, denials, and truths of their past and make sense of their present in ways that do not further compromise their dignity and wholeness. Without such meaningful engagement, it is unlikely that these youth will have the broad opportunities that full participation in our democratic society promises.

At the same time that high schools need to address these broader contexts of meaning making, they must also address a more immediate and concrete context: that of high school graduation. Although securing a diploma is a primary goal of high school, the path to it often has little meaning making opportunity. Particularly when students' school history is punctuated with disappointments, failures, or unusual hurdles, teaching and learning for making meaning requires teachers and schools to organize learning and curriculum so that students can organize knowledge in new ways to achieve the understanding and mastery that has previously eluded them. It means teaching those habits of work for school success and literacy and mathematics skills in ways that are personally relevant and engage student commitment to quality performance. After all, why should Hodgson students, who choose the school to avoid academics, want to develop intellectually? And what does Hodgson's instructional program do to enable students to find meaning in academic and intellectual engagement? What compels them to make commitments to academic work? What does the Urban Academy's educational program do to enable its students to find enough meaning in high school to commit themselves to meeting its rigorous demands and obtaining a diploma? How does International's instructional program enable its students to find meaning in their new culture, its history, its values, and demands?

A CLASSROOM FOR PUBLIC AND PERSONAL DISCOURSE

International High School presents one of the most challenging venues for teaching and learning for making meaning because its population of recent immigrant, new English language learners comes from a diverse group of nations, which range from emergent democracies to unstable or repressive dictatorships. Furthermore, they are not strangers to family separation and personal hardship. Nested in these complicated layers of multiple languages, widely diverse cultures, students' personal circumstances and levels and kinds of education, including interrupted schooling as well as vastly different degrees of understanding about American democracy, International's teachers find their way to teach for making meaning. Teachers build bridges, not only to English language proficiency and the complexities of American culture, but across students' diverse indigenous cultures. Where schools have traditionally sought to dissolve this rich and uniquely American cultural and linguistic diversity into a mythological melting pot, International High School strives to preserve its integrity as inherent to becoming American and capitalizes on it as a core feature of teaching and learning for making meaning. At International, becoming an American does not mean unbecoming who you were in another place at another time.

In a small windowless room, International High School Humanities teacher Harold Bretstein, known as Bret to students and colleagues, confronts the challenge of making U.S. culture and democracy and the values and subtleties embedded within them comprehensible and meaningful to his new American students. Bretstein's 24 students, seated around hexagonal tables in self-selected, ethnically and linguistically mixed groups of eight, open their looseleaf binders to display their homework. Fridays are current events day in Bretstein's Humanities class, and current events is one vehicle Bretstein uses to teach about American democracy and culture as it manifests itself in American and local foreign language newspaper articles and American newspaper political cartoons. The current events' homework task requires students to apply generic comprehension and analytic skills: from a native or English language paper they select an article on an important event, create their own headline, locate the story's setting, identify the key individuals and important details, summarize the article in English and their native language, and add personal comments.

At their tables in class, students take turns presenting their articles in both English and their native language. Although English is the language for public discourse at International, students use their native language as a tool for making meaning and a bridge to their new culture and language as well as the cultures and languages of their peers. Bretstein sees formal native language use as a vehicle for students' understanding and personal validation as well as building common ground across cultures:

> The use of native language helps them understand the content of the article better–as well as the English. . . . When the kids hear each other's native language it demystifies it. They can find similar words within their own language.

After each student's turn, his or her peers write a couple of sentences explaining what they think the article is about. They discuss their responses and then assess the student's presentation. Did the presentation enable them to understand the issues in the article? Was the quality of the presentation excellent? Good? Fair? Then the group as a whole grades the work.

Students' selection of articles reflects a broad range of interests and personal perspectives on what constitutes importance. Students' selections include a Spanish paper's story on President Bush's budget, a Russian paper's story of President Bush's meeting with Israeli Premier Ariel Sharon, a Korean paper's story of the Berenson trial in Peru, a Polish paper's story on Sean Puffy Combs, a Lebanese paper's story of the Taliban destruction of Buddha statues, a Chinese paper's story on Mayor Giuliani's plans to eliminate the Board of Education, a Spanish paper's story on a Brazilian oil rig, a Russian paper's story on student shootings in San Diego, and a New York *Daily News* story of the Roussini custody battle.

At one table, a tall, lanky Russian boy reads aloud his English summary of an article on the food wasted in local schools. He explains that the food cannot be saved for the following day because there is inadequate security to ensure its freshness. As a result, the excess food goes into a landfill. A better solution, he suggests, would be to give students second lunches, which is routinely denied to those who want one. Deciding to waste food instead of feeding hungry adolescents makes no sense. His peers agree. Following his explanation, he reads his summary in Russian.

Next a newly arrived Korean boy, who speaks very little English, nonetheless reads–anxiously–the English summary of his article, which is about the Berenson retrial in Peru. "He rarely speaks in class but the small group permits it without embarrassment," Bretstein later confides. A burly South American boy seated next to him helps him read and pronounce the words correctly in English so that others at the table can understand. The others, who speak Polish, Russian, and Spanish, also try to help. They are patient and good-humored as their Korean peer tries to explain the story in English. They ask him questions: "What did she [the Berensen girl] do?" When he has difficulty responding in English, another student explains that Berenson was a member of a terrorist group.

But a second student argues that it is not clear that Berensen was a member of a terrorist group. "You believe that!" challenges the first student.

"Where is proof?" the second student asks. They debate briefly as the Korean student returns to the article to locate its arguments.

The next presenting student begins with a question: "What do you think about classes on weekends?" Students give their opinions. His article is from a Spanish paper. He discusses its report on weekend schools in 26 of the 32 New York City school districts. The weekend schools hold classes for "struggling" students, "those who need the classes," he explains.

"This is happening already?" one girl asks.

"Yes," he says. "This is a good idea for students but you should not have to get up early on the weekends." Students debate whether Saturday or Sunday would be better for the classes, basing their opinions on their weekend schedules.

One girl has selected an article on the Roussini child custody battle initiated by a man completing a 10-year prison sentence. When Bretstein asks her what makes the article important, she asserts:

> A father is fighting for his kids. He has a right to raise his
> kids even if he was in prison. It doesn't mean he doesn't
> care about his kids. It shows he cares because he is fighting
> for them. And he has been away from them for a lotta years.
> He should have a chance with them. They should be with
> their father.

What at first seems like an "unimportant" event, more gossip than "news," turns out, upon the teacher's inquiry, to have a deeper meaning about attachment, love, and fairness.

Although many students have selected what would be considered conventionally important articles, others have selected articles that cover personally important issues in the context of their own adolescent lives: paternity, hunger, security, time, and school. The activity takes students across cultural boundaries by giving them common ground for conversation and opportunities to enact their multiple identities; although they are immigrants from different nations, they are adolescents, emergent Americans, and students in the same class, interdisciplinary cluster, and school. The activity enables them to express their ideas and opinions and challenge those of others and to make judgments on decisions that affect their lives. It reinforces the class as a diverse community and unifies them through the enactment of one of the most critical values and norms of their new culture—the use of English as a common language for public discourse and the free expression of multiple perspectives.

The second component of Friday's Current Events class is a political cartoon interpretation. Not only do political cartoons present a window into American culture; they are preparation for New York State Regents exams, which require students to interpret primary documents. Bretstein has selected a *Washington Post* cartoon (Carlson, Stuart. [3/27/01]. *The Washington Post.* http://www2.unclick.com/client/wpc/sc/) in which a group of parents seated in a living room debate multiple strategies for dealing with "all these school shootings." During the parents' discourse on increasing discipline, therapy, personal responsibility, counseling, and parent awareness, two tykes, unsupervised in an adjacent room, rifle through an open cabinet loaded with guns.

Students within each group share their interpretations of the cartoon. "Parents complain what they are going to do and they need more discipline, but the parents own guns," comments one student.

"Point," says a student in another group, "is that parents are not doing what they are talking about. What they are talking about is not going to stop the shootings. First, get rid of the guns in your house."

In the third group, a student explains, "Parents are saying that they have to be more aware about what is going on, but meanwhile their children are playing with guns in the next room." Although students in each group grasp the cartoon's irony, connections to the American context of the Second Amendment not surprisingly elude them. Bretstein's awareness of what levels of meaning students do and do not bring to their interpretations will inform the content of future lessons.

These images of Bretstein's class show how pedagogical choices, instructional practice, and curricular decisions create a variety of learning opportunities that evoke meaning making. Although students had diverse English language capacity, Bretstein held them to a common set of standards for the same task. He presented learning opportunities that evoked universal and diverse understandings and meanings of irony and symbols as well as more deeply constructed and personal meanings in the political interpretations. The tasks enabled students to practice the expression of the American value of multiple and conflicting perspectives without violence or repression. Because Bretstein's organization of learning tasks required students to use their native and new languages, interpret visual and print media, express themselves orally and in writing, work independently and in small groups, and assess one another according common criteria, they had a variety of opportunities to find their own as well as hear and understand others' meaning.

The nature of the tasks and choices also presented students with opportunities to develop their English and literacy skills, express their interests and their voice, to reveal what they think and believe (including their political opinions, which in some cases were critical of authority), and to defend their responses when challenged. These elements constitute what Bretstein's colleague Dina Heisler refers to "the habits of active citizenship" as they are lived in their new nation and as teachers hope students will live in their future.

How this pedagogy helps International's immigrant students make sense of and find direction in their new world is expressed in this student's comments:

> When I came here, I didn't really speak English. I did not
> know what the society is about. I did not know how it's like
> to be in America and how it's like to be in New York and
> how to find friends. I had this paranoid all kinds of things.
> And I was scared to meet people and make friends and
> speak English. This class helped me to adjust the things that
> were so new to me. . . in many ways to become involved in
> things.

HOW MAKING MEANING FINDS ITS WAY ONTO THE TEACHING AND LEARNING LANDSCAPE

The commitment to making meaning is pervasive on the three schools' landscape for teaching and learning. It inheres within their intentions, within their curriculum, instructional strategies, and classrooms and opportunity structures, which create the spaces for meaning making, and within the determination and capacity of teachers, who are the carriers of the opportunities for meaning making. It has both a personal, intellectual, and civic dimension. It is neither accidental nor incidental. This chapter will look at how teaching and learning for making meaning are operationalized in the schools.

Intentions for Making Meaning

The Urban Academy's commitment to teaching and learning for meaning making inheres in its vision as a "people-centered" educational community where inquiry and the engagement of multiple perspectives link students to the traditions of inquiry and its role in our democracy:

> Students seek understanding in the same way as inquiring minds have done over the centuries. They ask questions and examine the variety of ways they can be answered. . . . They become good citizens who value civil debate and can and will engage in making informed choices for our nation. (Urban Academy, 1993/1991)

Codirector Herb Mack explained: "We want students to learn that in our democratic society, reasonable people, given the same evidence, can and will come up with diametrically opposed interpretations, and that's OK."

The value system at International, as Heisler explained, links learning to make sense of oneself and the world and making the world and oneself make sense, to identity development, human wholeness, and social responsibility:

> One of the [school] values is for students to become self-actualized human beings—people who feel that they have power in the world, who take charge; thinking people, who can evaluate and give real good, critical thought to what's going on and around them, and humanist values, treasuring other people. It's not just the skills, like being able to stand up and do public speaking or to order an agenda. It's the kind of interaction and the feeling that they matter, they count (see Appendix, Exhibit 3).

Hodgson links meaning making to its mission to develop students to be productive individuals and citizens through (among other practices) the use of multiple forms of assessment that legitimize diversity and enable students to demonstrate their productivity and achievement in multiple, authentic, and unconventional as well as conventional ways. As a result, students learn that capacity, academic achievement, and productivity can be meaningfully expressed in ways other than on standardized tests. In a high-stakes tests environment, these opportunities for multiple forms of expression are important because, as one student said: "Some people don't test well."

Explained another, "What's on a piece of paper is not what you are. You have to show yourself." Hodgson students have multiple opportunities to "show" themselves as productive achievers–in their career class products; community internships; and academic classroom projects, simulations, and exhibitions. These opportunities for students to express their achievements in multiple ways keep tests from becoming silencing mechanisms for students who show what they know and can do in ways uncommon to school tradition. Hodgson's academic and vocational performance assessments release students from the repressive grip of the one-size-fits-all assessments that in fact don't fit them to reimagine themselves and their possibilities and their worth. Since the inception of Hodgson's academic-vocational integration reform, increasing numbers of students see themselves as having academic capacity and apply for and are accepted at postsecondary school education institutions, despite static SAT scores.

Curriculum for Making Meaning

In order to support the engagement necessary for making meaning, the faculty of each school design curriculum to appeal to their particular student population and themselves and also align with the learning standards set by their state. To reengage their disaffected students, UA faculty design "a spread of courses [that] will deepen the students' understanding of topics which already interest them and expose them to ideas, issues, and information that are new" (*Urban Academy* 1994b, p. 1). Courses reflect not only students' interests and learning needs, but the multiple investments of diverse stakeholders: that is, faculty members' interests, passions, and talents; UA's pedagogical and social ethos; and UA and the state's graduation requirements (See Appendix, Exhibit 4).

In thematic English courses, UA adolescents can channel their personal struggles into a rigorous and disciplined inquiry of literature to make meaning of their own life experiences, as well as expand their exploration of broader intellectual themes. Examples include "Misfits in Literature," in which students examine the theme of alienation and the social marginalization of individuals who are different by reading and discussing novels such as *The Hunchback of Notre Dame, The Heart is a Lonely Hunter,* and *Frankenstein.* "O Brother! O Sister?" is a course in which students probe conflicts between siblings by studying Biblical stories, contemporary literature, and psychological theories. In the course "Raising Ourselves," students examine the theme of parental abandonment from the perspective of youth.

In social studies and arts courses, UA students explore and make sense of societal and historical problems and contradictions that concern them. In the class "Social Documentary Photography," students observe a self-selected aspect of society through "the lens of the camera and the photographer's eye" (Urban Academy, 2001, p. 10). In UA's American History course, students explore "how history is made by examining what [democracy, freedom, and power] meant to different groups of people during the Civil War and Reconstruction" (Urban Academy, 2001, p. 2). Particular focus is given to multiple perspectives on "who or what was responsible for the end of slavery, the degree to which former slaves and other 'ordinary' Americans were capable of managing their own lives and running governments" (Urban Academy, 2001, p. 2).

Courses that bring teachers' interests, talents, and passions to the classroom occur in all content areas, and include "A History of the Civil Rights Movement," "The Economics of Money," "Law," "Puzzles" (a course in code breaking, riddles, mini-mysteries, mazes, and scientific, topological, and mathematical puzzles), and "Opera," where students study operas and attend dress rehearsals and full performances at the Metropolitan Opera House at Lincoln Center. Courses such as "Latin American Fiction," in which students read and analyze short and long works by Latin American writers such as Gabriel Garcia Marquez; or "Love and Conflict in Literature," in which students read fiction of different genres from ancient Greece to the 20th Century to explore how lovers across time and cultures have coped with social taboos; and "Introduction to African American Literature" all enact the Urban Academy's multicultural ethos.

Courses to support students' skill development are also designed to be intellectually engaging and challenging. "Novels: Getting to Like

Them," aims to help students who lack success in reading novels find meaning and pleasure in tackling them. The syllabus features high-interest novels designed to capture and sustain students' interest so that they develop confidence in their capacity to read a long work to completion. Another such course, "Children's Books: Are They for Children?," enables students of diverse reading levels to participate equally in sophisticated analyses of issues such as class, gender, and race as they are treated in the texts and illustrations of children's books. Although UA courses are an unconventional organization of the curriculum for high school, they align completely with the New York state standards.

Hodgson's curricular decisions aim to encourage academically ambivalent students to find meaning in academic pursuit. Faculty designed the Senior Project research paper so that students choose a vocational topic of interest in their career major. The shop focus and the opportunity for student choice generate task motivation. Jason, a Culinary student, remarked:

> Because you are doing it in your shop area, you want to do
> it even more. The reason why I like the Senior Project is
> they gave you the opportunity to pick it yourself. They
> didn't say, "You have to do this. You have to do that." They
> told us to write down five topics you like and pick whichever
> you liked best. So I picked chicken–the poultry industry of
> Delaware.

Although students select the topics, teachers review them to ensure that they stretch students intellectually. Frank, a Plumbing student, explained: "The topic you pick for your Senior Project's got to be something that you've learned in the three years that you've been in shop [but] something you don't know about and want to. And it's big."

Another remarks on the project's demand for synthesis: "It is all your own ideas but you have to put them together."

The comments of another student let us see how the design element of choice links pleasure, task commitment, and responsibility to stimulate motivation: "You have fun because you can think about what you want to do, how you want to do it. You control how it goes."

The assumptions of Hodgson faculty that students bring something of value to contribute to the curriculum and that they will make responsible choices pay off. Students' contributions personalize the curriculum, and that personalization contributes to their task commitment. Despite

initial student threats about transferring to other schools if the Senior
Project research paper was required, all Hodsgon seniors do in fact complete it. The project's enduring success led the staff to petition the district to make the Senior Project a graduation requirement, thereby raising the school's standards for a high school diploma. Not surprisingly,
since the inception of its own higher standards, Hodgson's high postsecondary school-going and low graduates' unemployment rates have dis-
tinguished it from the other schools in its district.

The integration of academic and vocational education curriculum
has also promoted teaching and learning for making meaning.
Maintenance Technology teacher Dale Derrickson claims that "using the
trade as the foundation to teach math concepts gets students' interest."
In the Math Integration Initiative there is a reciprocal integration of
mathematics and vocational education curriculum. Shop and Math
teachers seek appropriate opportunities for integration in their respec-
tive content areas. Math teachers find ways to refer to students' shop
experiences and integrate shop terminology into their lessons.

Math teacher Darnell Grandell explained: "When we were talking
about such things as the slope of a line in Algebra, we could refer to the
pitch of a roof," a Carpentry term.

Derrickson contends that math integration made math more relevant and important to students by generating "a need to know":

> [It] shows them that math is really important in what they've
> got to do. . . . They see the need for the application of math.
> It's not just that you have to learn how to do this because it's
> on the next page in the book and we just finished the last
> page. It's something where they can say, "Hey, I might need
> to know to do that."

Students' need to know, coupled with the knowledge that there is
a way to know what they need, has generated excitement about mathematics learning. Math teacher Janet Ryer recounted, "One day last
week, students ran down to my room and said, 'We need you on
Wednesday to help us do conversions.' They seemed pretty excited
about it. They really wanted to know how to do it."

The two courses that constitute Hodgson's Principles of
Technology initiative enable Hodgson students to apply physics to their
career major. Students apply concepts in physics and math-related-

physics to science projects in which they explore the principles of force, resistance, energy, waves, and momentum, which are related to mechanical, electrical, fluid, thermal radiation, and optical systems. Students do some of the science projects in their shops. Dave Lutz explained, "The science, math, and vocational concepts all run together." If students pass both courses, they obtain credit for one physics course.

Derrickson finds the science and vocational education curricula naturally compatible:

> In maintenance technology, students study plumbing. There's a science unit [on] thermodynamics. One is a heating science unit that has a lot of physics: the characteristics of fluid flow and fluid motion, expansion of fluids. This is actually convection flow for heating, but it's all science. A lot of the science has math in it, too. This is also plumbing science.
>
> I also have a plumbing English unit where [students] have to write a story about what happens when a hot water heater blows up. They have to grasp the math that goes along with this, too. [They have to] determine the calculations, interpolate a chart, and do the science of why you get this super-heated fluid. Then they have to write about it. . . . The English teachers have offered to grade it for the English part. I've been grading it for the content.

Traditional conceptualizations of curriculum also present challenges for teaching and learning for making meaning at International. In particular, humanities teachers confront what teacher Kathy Fine describes as "the American point of identification," common in typical Social Studies texts, and their assumption of a native-born American audience steeped in a hegemonic perspective of American culture. Fine and colleagues contend that immigrant students can frequently find their native country, culture, and people demonized or denigrated in traditional American History texts and tests. Characterizations of American-Soviet/Russian relations through cartoons such as a world split between Uncle Sam on the American continent and an ominous bear on the Russian continent or Jingoistic explanations of laws such as the Chinese Exclusion Act can confuse and pain immigrant students from those nations, most of whom still have family in their countries of origin.

Additionally, argues Dina Heisler, such curriculum and texts teach an "uncritical view [of history] that encourages students to be passive receptors of received wisdom." In contrast, she and her colleagues want students to:

> Learn how history is constructed–look at the various biases–
> be historiographers–examine primary sources–look at what
> the conflicts were over–what the issues were–the flash points
> in American history. Looking at things from the perspective
> of conflict raises other voices and mirrors what is happening
> today. It also deals with the resolutions to these conflicts.
> Did they leave residue that we are still grappling with today?
> Who were winners and losers? Then you can see the con-
> nections between past and what we are seeing around us.

Such an approach provides students with the opportunity to make connections between the past and the present, increasing their stake in their learning because it relates to their lives.

Heisler's beliefs, which are very compatible with International's commitment to teaching students social responsibility, led her and her team to the American Social History Project, where they found curriculum that reflected their and the school's educational commitments to equity, social justice, critical thinking, and adolescent development. In social history, said Heisler:

> History is the history of everyone. It is important to bring in
> the forgotten voices–women, people of color–and to show
> how all were agents of change. It also looks at historiogra-
> phy. Then [using the American Social History Project], you
> have a student-centered classroom, which is important
> because what does it mean that ordinary people make histo-
> ry if students are disempowered?

In the American Social History Project, the story of the United States prominently features the historical perspectives, voices, and contributions of the diverse social, ethnic, and racial groups that are usually marginalized in society and in the curriculum. The project's materials include firsthand accounts of historical events and episodes (such as immigration, the labor movement, and enslavement) from multiple perspectives, as well as visuals and fictional interpretations of life for diverse Americans.

Heisler's students have examined different "visions of America" by analyzing and discussing literature with different perspectives on America. One time they compared Langston Hughes's *Let America Be America Again* with Emma Lazarus's *The New Colossus: Inscription for the Statue of Liberty* to see what is true about America and for whom. Such analyses and class discussions liberate students to share and examine their own experiences, help them understand the experiences of others, validate their differences, and consider the meaning and consequences of those differences.

Bridging the past and the present and connecting her immigrant students to their new and complex American nation stimulates Heisler to improvise, and at International, teacher improvisation is encouraged. One day she brought to class three *New York Times* articles which, juxtaposed with each other, made a powerful statement on American diversity. In one article, a Thai woman brought to the United States for a job was enslaved into prostitution. Another article reported on a White man who had just bought a company, using money he had inherited from his family. The third article told of an African-American reporter for the *Wall Street Journal* and his mother who, after one of their tokens got stuck, went through a subway turnstile together, were arrested, and had to spend the night in jail. They had been rushing home after he had taken her to a Broadway show.

The class discussion of the lives of the people in the articles became an investigation into class and caste in America. Students inquired into the history of racism and immigration and the lives of immigrants—and the ways in which immigrants are vulnerable. By examining what it means to come from the dominant culture and to have inherited wealth, students explored the intersection of class and caste, what that means to them individually, and how people's points of view are shaped by where they come from—that is, their class and caste. They looked at whether there is class mobility in America and what can be changed. They looked at who the people are who can define themselves and who the people are who are defined by others, who has the advantage and the power in the process of mobility, what the struggles are to realize the promise of the American Revolution, and how we as a nation can fulfill that promise. They looked at how the American Revolution is still going on.

Instruction for Making Meaning

Similarly to the schools' curriculum, their instructional approaches map onto their mission and operationalize their commitments. Inquiry learning at the Urban Academy is

> an environment which promotes active learning and critical thinking. At its core is an emphasis on . . . helping students to use their mind well, on encouraging students to grapple with authentic, often controversial questions. Primary source materials, not textbooks, are used extensively. Informed discussion requiring the use of evidence and exposure to conflicting ideas occurs across subject disciplines. The goal of the school is to create a rigorous academic community in which students assume increasing responsibility for their learning. . . . Often, work assignments require cooperation and peer collaboration. (*Background,* no date, no pages)

We see this vision operating in the school's classrooms. In a class about the meaning of life in Mack's "Issues" course, students asked sophisticated and complex personal questions such as, How do you believe in something you can't see? On what do you base your decisions to determine what you believe in when everyone looks at reality in a different way? Were the first 4 days [in the Biblical creation myth] what we know as days? These questions both emerged from and generated class discussion. In science teacher Barry Fox's "Evolution" course, students used evidence and documentation to analyze an argument on the origins of life.

During a lengthy class discussion on the question, "Is the federal government established by the American founders relevant and equipped to respond to current problems emblemized by the Rodney King case?", students in Barlowe's American History course challenged the accuracy of each other's facts and interpretations.

Although UA's inquiry pedagogy is characterized by the particular set of features described above, teachers design instruction with their particular students in mind so that it

> incorporates values and experiences of the individual student [in order to] give immediate context to new knowledge. For example, student analysis of current events may have deep meaning for students whose lives are affected daily by contemporary problems such as urban violence. (Urban Academy, 1994a, p. 3)

When teachers make instructional choices based on who their students are, it influences their engagement. One student explained: "You're not just listening to a teacher lecture you. You're talking to other kids your age."

The descriptions of instruction by several students explain the role of public discussion in facilitating meaning making. Students learn to take a stand and defend their perspective, hear perspectives different from their own, and honor the "no personal attacks" rule, which stipulates that they may attack ideas but not people. Assignments demand that students articulate their thinking coherently, persuasively, and publicly. One student said, "[The work] forces you to get your thoughts out in the open. You learn to get your point of view across."

Another remarked: "You have to explain yourself. [The teachers are] not going to let you off if you don't explain yourself. You have to make yourself clear."

Another explained the expectations for supporting opinions with evidence:

> You have to think for yourself. You have to research so you
> understand what you're talking about because when you get
> into class, and you want to give your opinion, you have to
> be able to back it up.

Another explained the effects that taking ideas seriously has had on her:

> I can honestly listen to other people's opinions. I wouldn't
> really listen before. I thought I was right and there was no
> other way of looking at [an issue]. At UA I learned that you
> can disagree without disrespecting.

By making disciplined student voice an integral part of instruction, students understand how they influence the quality of instruction in their classes. One student said:

> At Urban, it's not always necessarily the teachers that make
> the class interesting. If you have an opinion and say it, and
> no one responds to it, the class would not be a class. . . .
> [But] because you're putting a part of yourself into the class
> discussion, you're kinda deciding what's gonna be taught in

that class. If you bring something up, then that's what we're
gonna discuss.

Cook believes that the most powerful impact of UA's inquiry
approach to learning is its ecouragement of students to develop their
voice: "They know they are listened to. It is empowering."

Warshawsky's classes present images of how UA's inquiry
approach promotes meaning making in mathematics. Students, organized into small, heterogeneous problem-solving groups of two to five,
work collaboratively on math problems. Simultaneous to their small-
group interaction, some students talk out to Warshawsky as though they
are thinking aloud. Some students talk to Warshawsky across the room
while others talk up close. They explain to him what they are doing to
solve the problem, asking for his intervention when they get stuck.
When students were measuring the central angle in a Geometry class,
several called out to Warshawsky: "Could you have done it his way?
This way?" At all times knowing who was asking what question,
Warshawsky gave reassurance when needed, assistance in the form of
questions when students lost their way, and context when one student
questioned the relevance of the activities. The main thrust always, as
Warshawsky says, "is for the student to prove to his or her teammates
that the answer makes sense."

Warshawsky feels that this dynamic, learner-centered, teacher-
facilitated problem-solving approach to mathematics respects the
uneven learning rates and diverse learning patterns and capacities of students and enables them to understand what they are doing and make
meaning in their idiosyncratic ways. He resists feeding them formulas
for solving problems because he wants them to develop and internalize
feelings of capacity and confidence, to "feel able to approach problems,
to try them, when no teacher is around."

He believes that the group work provides students with opportunities to discover their own idiosyncratic strategies for locating patterns,
generating formulas, and solving math problems as well as learning that
the strategies of their peers are also idiosyncratic. There is no one right
way, and he believes the ways in which students solve problems are
characteristic of the work habits of real-life mathematicians. By organizing an authentic problem-solving environment, where all the class rules
reinforce persistence, curiosity, challenge, and teamwork, Warshawsky
hopes his classes make math accessible to his students and his students

accessible to the possibilities of mathematics.

Kathleen, who failed New York State's "Sequential Mathematics I" course three times, explained that UA's learning conditions and pedagogy provided her with the opportunity to find her way through the algebra curriculum and generated the self-confidence and learning that made the difference between a high level of performance and failure:

> When I first did algebra in ninth grade [in her former school] I got a 59. Last term, I did the same exact algebra and got a 96. It's not about not understanding it. It's about when someone rushes you and makes you feel stupid, you're never going to do good because you don't think you can. And when someone thinks you can do it, of course you can do it; it's very simple. "Look. Here we go! You can do it this way. You can do it that way. . . ." You see all your options and you don't feel pressured into doing it like every other student in the school–of course you can do well.
>
> With Wally you can learn different ways. It's not set. I couldn't get math by teachers' lecturing and copying from the board and memorizing. In a group someone can show me. I can see what others are doing. I can understand that. And I'm going to have a whole hour so I'll have the time. And I can be with somebody to help me find where I'm stuck. With Wally you can say at any point, "I'm not getting it. What do I do here?" And you're not afraid for Wally to feel that you're stupid. You're not afraid because kids at Urban ask questions. You're not getting taught in one way. Everybody at Urban knows there's different ways of learning. . . . We work as a team, so no one's going to put someone down.

Collaborative activity-based learning is also a central feature of International's instructional strategy to promote meaning making. This instructional approach operationalizes the school's mission to promote intellectual development, social responsibility, the "linguistic, cognitive, and cultural skills necessary for [students'] success in high school, college, and beyond" (International High School, 1985) as well as the school's beliefs that "learning is a social activity and knowledge, the out-

come of interactions among individuals [and] that everyone has something to offer" (International High School, 1993, p. 8).

What International means by social responsibility is that students
are responsible for one another's learning as well as their own. Since
making meaning is socially constructed, International students work collaboratively in groups. Tasks are organized for interdependency and
individual cooperation is required for groups to complete and obtain
credit for tasks. Within groups students regularly read one another's
work to assess correctness and quality and to suggest revisions. They
divide tasks for more in-depth study, as in an assignment to compare
and contrast the ideas of Langston Hughes, Pastor Niemoeller (a Nazi
victim), and Adlai Stevenson on social conflict, social responsibility, and
civil liberties.

The social contract embedded in collaborative learning, explained
Steve Lindberg, Social Studies and Math teacher, increases knowledge
for all:

> [The point of group work] is to gain knowledge and mastery
> over a certain amount of material and then exchange it with
> each other or impart it to the rest of the class. Each person
> has to carry a fair share or not only are they hurting them-
> selves, not only are they hurting the entire group, but [they
> are] taking away from the depth of knowledge that the rest
> of the class is going to get. Looking at it from the other point
> of view, each person is benefiting by the work that the other
> kids are doing. So you're actually not just cheating yourself
> by not doing the work, but you're cheating the entire class.

Teacher-developed student activity guides for each interdisciplinary team contain a sequence of activities at diverse levels of intellectual challenge, which lead individual students and the groups through
required tasks. Teachers and students negotiate the levels of challenge
that students choose depending on their collaborative judgment of the
group's capacity to support them and the degree of frustration the
teacher thinks will be productive in achieving the learning goals.
Because the process constructs an agreement among the teacher, individuals, and the group, it supports task commitment.

International's teachers claim that activity-based learning changes
the nature of teaching by encouraging teachers to center their instruction

on the needs of learners and focus on how students are making sense (or not) of the learning tasks. Biology teacher Alison McCluer remarked:

> Rather than us being at the board talking to the students, we're walking around looking at what the students are doing, working with them, showing them things, and observing what they're doing. So we see day-to-day exactly what the student is doing. We can see what they have trouble with when they started and we can see what they're trying to do about it. We can see if they're trying to avoid tasks. We can see if they're making movement from tasks. It's really hard to miss what the students are doing because they're always working.

Because "teaching is subordinated to learning" (International High School, 1993, p. 8), teachers are expected to enter into the learning experiences of the student for their teaching cues. Teachers have to make sense of how students are making meaning of their challenges. One strategy teachers use is known as "debriefing." Debriefing enables teachers to ascertain the ways in which and the depth to which individual students and their groups are understanding instructional experiences and concepts they are encountering. These "Socratic conversations" often begin with the teacher asking a simple definition question and progressing to more sophisticated questions that require individuals and the group to apply their learnings. Because debriefings inform teachers of what students know, how they have come to know it, and what they need to know, follow-up activities that deepen and expand students' understanding can be customized to specific student and group needs. Strategies such as debriefing support meaning making as a norm of professional teaching practice that directs teachers' focus on learning for understanding.

Hodgson also uses collaborative, activity-based instruction to support task commitment and meaning making. As one student reported, collaboration expands students' knowledge:

> We often get in groups of four [and] we work together. . . . In some classes we make webs where you come up with a topic. If you were in history, your topic could be Japan. We brainstorm facts on the topic like you could put ten things

outside of the web that would say, like, Japan had bombed Pearl Harbor on such and such a date. It's everybody helping one another.

Another explained the problem-solving support provided by small group collaboration:

In my Math class last year, we always worked in groups. At the beginning of the year, most of us didn't know what we were doing but by the middle of the year, we all knew what we were doing because we all helped each other if we had a problem. . . .

Mark Grandell found that project-based learning that took students into some depth not only increased student commitment; it encouraged intellectual development and higher performance standards more than rote kinds of activities:

I found the level of [student] productivity—the quality and volume of work—doing the projects is higher than the times when we're not. If we go back into the textbook to do a more traditional lesson over an extended period of time, the productivity seems to drop off. [On the projects] students concentrated on the process of getting the answer. When we did the textbooks, they tended not to show their work and to follow a logical sequence of pattern. They just wanted to put down the answer. I think the project has some type of ownership in it. I think there is a sense of pride in a finished product that is tangible, more than a set of problems in a book.

[On the projects] we try to help students to learn to use their minds well. We ask open-ended questions. We allow for library time for research on each of our particular projects. The librarian helps them with computer networking and their research skills. She prepares lists of references that might be appropriate for their project. We get them to answer particular questions in written form where they discuss and explain rather than just calculate a particular answer.

Hodgson's math integration initiative has spawned "need-to-know" instruction, which encourages making meaning of mathematics through its application to that which is important and immediately relevant to students—their shop projects—in a context that matters and makes sense to them—their shops. Ryer, Darnell Grandell, and Derrickson asserted that the opportunity to provide math instruction in response to students' particular needs showed them the benefits of math in ways that learning math in isolation could not.

"Need-to-know" instruction liberates the knowledge and skills needed to solve a particular problem from the official curricular scope and sequences so that they become accessible to students at a time that they are meaningful to their learning. Ryer said, "Students get the math they need at the time they need it in their shop which they might not get—like the trig—until their senior year."

Such instruction helps students understand their learning challenges more broadly, as in the case of this carpentry student who described how Darnell Grandell had recently helped him not only with the math he needed but also to determine the root cause of the problem he was encountering:

> Miss Grandell came down [to the shop] and helped with
> the math problems that came up with the roofing. There
> were problems [with] the measurements and angles. . . .
> She helped with math figures. She made sure I was still in
> the right, see what the problem really was—if it was me
> doing the math, or was it measuring or was it the roof
> itself.

In Derrickson's class, some of the math teachers pulled a group of students aside and taught them the math unit that corresponded with the shop. Ryer did the same in the Visual Communications Shop. She helped students use proportion to enlarge a small picture onto a grid. Ryer worked alongside five students, each of whom worked on a separate picture, cutting the grids into parts and transferring from the grid onto the picture. She helped them understand that if they doubled the length and width, they would make the picture four times as big, not twice as big. They talked about how changes in length and width change the area, how they have to change the length and width in the same proportion if they want to keep the final picture in the same proportion, and how they can change the proportion of the picture if they make the proportions different from what they originally were.

In technical drafting shop, Ryer taught small groups the reciprocal conversion of inches and millimeters and how to use fractions and a ruler. She connected mastery of basic skills to creativity: "Some of them got so creative and very into it in the tech drafting class, because you really need to know how to go from millimeters to inches." She worked with students on the math needed for bar graphs and pie charts, made them three dimensional, and found creative ways to present them so that students could express their uniqueness.

Darnell Grandell taught elementary trigonometry to a group of students in Carpentry because "they don't always get it in their regular math class or it's not taught when they're doing certain projects." She taught the algebra steps involved in the electric trades. In the Horticulture shop, she found an opportunity to teach skills.

Some teachers have applied the math integration "need-to-know" instructional strategy to their academic interdisciplinary clusters. Mark Grandell teaches math needed for science activities:

> I teach the math skills needed for students to do the science projects. In the egg drop project, I taught math related to rate, distance, time, and volume. For the steamboat project, I taught students how to find the volume of a particular amount of water.

Others teach scientific notation and algebra.

Not only has "need-to-know" instruction made mathematics more accessible and meaningful to students and increased their math knowledge, skills, and capacity, it has brought them closer to their math teachers. Darnell Grandell said, "The students love having the math teacher in shop."

Ryer agreed: "It becomes a personal thing. They really look forward to this because if I'm not there, they'll say, 'Where were you yesterday?'"

Stronger bonds among the members of the school community build the school's social capital, broadening the space for teachers to expand students' learning beyond their self-imposed limits.

INSTRUCTIONAL INFRASTRUCTURE
TO SUPPORT TEACHING AND LEARNING
FOR MAKING MEANING

Designing curriculum and instruction so that students have opportunities to make meaning and commitments does not mean that students have the skills or knowledge or will to effectively engage in those opportunities. Just because a school provides students with opportunities to express their points of view and make arguments for them doesn't mean they want or know how to do it in a disciplined and meaningful way that produces knowledge and understanding. Just because a school assigns a challenging research paper doesn't mean that students want to do it or know how to do it, and will produce a research paper of quality. Just because a school organizes learning for student collaboration does not mean that students want to or know how to work in groups or will work productively in groups to produce new knowledge, understanding, or quality work. Indeed, in addition to insufficient know-how, student resistance to these learning demands is not uncommon.

In order to help students achieve the necessary know-how and will to fully and successfully meet the demands to make meaning, each school has developed a support infrastructure that consists of proactive, curriculum-embedded, and responsive interventions. Hodgson's catalogue of best practices (see Appendix, Exhibit 5), their "need-to-know" courses, and curriculum to develop the capacity and skills students need to complete the Senior Project research paper exemplify proactive interventions. These interventions anticipate students' learning needs. They are based on teachers' knowledge of students and what they need in order to perform. Hodgson faculty do not wait until students are failing; they use their knowledge of students' work habits to structure the Senior Project experience for success and the prevention of failure. Proactive interventions include scaffolding, such as 9th and 10th grade intensive writing curriculum across the content areas, 11th grade curriculum units on oral presentations that prepare students for their Senior Project oral defenses, and the senior year technical writing course. At the time students *need to know* how to write a research paper for the Senior Project, the technical writing course teaches students how to write it, including the conventions of research such as taking notes on index cards, making citations correctly, compiling a bibliography, using multiple sources and forms of information, using multiple formats to present data (such as visuals and diagrams), and constructing a table of contents. A file of former Senior Project papers is available to help students understand what is expected of them (Darling-Hammond, Ancess, & Falk, 1995).

In an interview, plumbing student Frank described how he learned to write his Senior Project research paper:

> Well first [Ms. Steinwedel] presented [a] packet to us at the beginning of the year. Then she went over the whole thing. She, like, helped us through, step by step, like the paper first, and then tell you how to do it and the bibliographies and all that. [She explained] a way to research and get your information and put it all together to make a research paper. It's not complicated. Like somebody didn't know about a water well [Frank's project] could go in and read this [his research paper] and learn off of it. It ain't real complicated or nothing. Plain everyday talk.

Additionally, Hodgson uses its fiscal resources to offer Saturday Academy and Tuesday and Thursday tutoring, at which faculty provide enrichment, tutoring, and make-up sessions.

The Urban Academy's lab classes are similar proactive interventions. Lab courses are one-period attachments to intellectually challenging courses taught by someone other than the course teacher. Avram Barlowe calls them "supply-side courses [because] they teach students how to do the assignments for another teacher." They scaffold students' learning by supplying them with the interventions, skills, and supports necessary for school success. Students learn the conventions of writing, such as the proper use of quotations, the organization skills for constructing a coherent paper, perseverance for rewriting, and the struggle for finding their voice–figuring out what they want to say and crafting ways in which to say it. Labs are attached to courses that require students to read extensively and write analytic papers. These courses include "History of the Civil Rights Movement," "American History," "The Economics of Money," "Latin American Fiction," "Dostoyevsky," and "Poetry Workshop," the last in which students read and analyze poetry and write original poems.

Barlowe, Nancy Jachim, and Cook explained that labs increase students' access to courses with complex content by teaching them the demands of rigorous coursework while simultaneously providing them with opportunities to become proficient in those skills and habits necessary for meeting those demands. Without the labs, asserts Cook, many of the courses offered by UA would intimidate many UA students, demand more than they are capable of producing, require UA to lower their performance standards, or restrict enrollment to those few students who already have the skills necessary to meet the course demands.

UA and International explicitly teach curriculum units on the use of the library, which students *need to know* in order to do research required of them. UA organizes the course as a scavenger hunt, which sends students to the public libraries across the city to locate primary source materials, periodicals, and scientific abstracts to complete particular tasks.

International's teachers teach courses on leadership, group dynamics, and peer mediation, which students *need to know* to effectively collaborate. They also teach explicit lessons on how to work in groups. Steve Lindberg explained the necessity of such instruction:

> You have to show the kids how to work in groups. A lot of them come from schools where everybody's individual and there are thirty people in the class and the people only talk to the teacher. If they talk to the person next to them, they get punished for that. There is a fair amount of training: dividing up the work as equally as possible but taking into consideration the abilities of the different people in the group. Some people are much better at visual things, etcetera. We try to point out those things.

Learning how to work in groups mediates the ambivalence many International students have about collaborative learning. Such ambivalence generates anxiety about producing high-quality work, conflict over the uneven distribution of student capacity and motivation, self-interest, and a struggle to become a high-functioning group. Students like group learning when their group cooperates and when it advances their own individual learning. However, students are not necessarily eager to take the time to help their peers, although they all appreciate receiving help from their peers. These courses that teach students the technical knowledge and skills required for effective collaborative learning help them see its benefits and frustrations and exert some control. Some students discover and develop their leadership capacity. Others learn that collaboration can produce a better product than an individual endeavor.

Course- and project-embedded mechanisms help students organize their work, maintain time lines, and stay on task. Hodgson teachers developed a time-management chart that sequences the Senior Project's tasks with corresponding due dates and actual submission dates to help students manage their time. The list of concrete tasks, such as Working Bibliography, Note Cards, Advisor Interview (Consultation #1), First Draft, and Final Draft provide a secure structure that guides students through the project. Students mention that the time-management form and process keep them focused, and that they work from task to task, which makes the project doable for them. Teachers have organized the project to align with what students need to succeed.

Within courses at International, students formally reflect on and analyze their group process in order to improve their collaboration. One such activity guides students through a rigorous analysis of their group work:

> What happened in the group that caused the work to get done? What problems did the group have and how did you solve them? If you didn't solve them what ideas do you have on how they could have been solved? When you work with a group again, what would you like to do differently to make the group work its best? (Rugger, 1991, pp. 17–18)

Revision, which is a pervasive practice across the three schools, enables students to deepen their meaning-making experiences. For the course exhibitions and performance assessments required by each of the schools, students are expected to do multiple revisions of their work in response to written teacher critiques and conferences targeted to improving its quality. With each revision and with the oral presentations and defenses that accompany these exhibitions and performance assessments, students deepen their content understanding, clarify the meaning of their ideas, and develop an understanding of what constitutes quality work, and the kind of effort required to produce quality work as well as confidence in their capacity to produce it. One UA student commented:

> I've had papers handed back to me four, five, and six times. I've written papers over and over. [At UA] you get it pound-

ed into you. You have teachers who insist deeply that you write your paper correctly, organize your thoughts.

Another said, "My work habits are improving and I'm slowly edging my way towards that big research paper. I'm kinda scared sometimes, but I feel more confident."

A Hodgson student whose performance assessment was on scratchboard propaganda explained the impact the revision process had on his learning:

> You think more. . . . You learn a lot more. . . . My topic was scratchboard propaganda. It was a futuristic look at propaganda. I never, never knew anything about propaganda–never heard of it, nothing. It made me learn a lot about real war. It made me think about what they thought back then in World War I and World War II. [Also] Vietnam–I read a little bit on that. . . . I learned about scratchboarding and artists that did scratchboarding. I learned about the paper shortage back in those days. I never heard anything about that, nothing about that.

Responsive mechanisms, that is, mechanisms that are triggered when problems emerge, include teacher and peer tutoring, teacher-student conferences, and informal teacher-student encounters made possible by teachers' close relationships with and intimate knowledge of students and the easy access teachers and students have to each other. To problem-solve students' predicaments, UA faculty engages in a staff review process and International's teacher teams use a case approach. In both instances faculty describe student behavior, analyze it, brainstorm remedies, and plan for their application.

TEACHER LEARNING

If a school is going to be committed to teaching and learning for making meaning, then teachers must have opportunities to make meaning in their work; for engaged, challenged, and committed learning and learners will not come from rote teaching or robotic teachers constrained from interpreting students' behavior, or improvising to capitalize on a "teachable moment," or applying their tacit knowledge or professional learnings and judgments. Making sense and meaning of how and what one's students are learning, interpreting what students' responses and behavior mean, and using this information to inform one's practice—that is, making choices, decisions, and judgments about curriculum, learning activities, assessments, classroom organization, interventions, and responses—are at the heart of effective teaching.

The structure of teachers' work in the three schools encourages and sets the expectation for teachers to make sense of their teaching and students' learning and to make their work meaningful, connected to them and their school's beliefs and knowledge. Teachers have regular time blocks to meet and collaborate with their colleagues and to review, critically reflect upon, and correct their practice. They serve on committees that make decisions about curriculum, instruction, assessment, and student interventions. They design the courses and the curriculum they teach. They have opportunities to teach courses that embody their interests and passions, even when they are not in their license area and even when there is no license for them. They make decisions about time allocation for instruction and students' work. They decide with whom they will team and who will teach in their school. Teachers' involvement in their school's decision-making invests them in the culture and effectiveness of their work, their students' work, and the work of the school. If their practice isn't working, they change it; if school isn't working, they change it. Faculty are continuously changing their practice and their school for greater efficacy and quality. All of these activities engage teachers in struggles within themselves and among themselves but they also generate meaning in teaching work. Furthermore, teachers' involvement in their school strengthens their commitments to it. Teachers do what is necessary to get students to learn and to make the school work for the school community.

Of particular importance and uniqueness are the opportunities these schools provide for teachers to apply what they learn from their practice and to make it public so that the benefits are equitably accessible and can be distributed across the school. As teachers understand students' responses to their instruction, they transform their practice to be in closer alignment with their new knowledge about what their students need in order to achieve the course and school goals. Teachers have the freedom and authority to act on the meaning they are making of what is occurring in their classes.

We see how this process works in each of the schools. UA's Barlowe transformed the school's college-course advisory class into the college homework lab, inventing UA's first lab course. As UA's liaison for its collaboration with a local community college at which UA students were enrolled in actual college courses, Barlowe observed that UA students needed help analyzing the assignments, organizing and drafting their work, managing their time, and persisting in the face of frustration. As he learned what students' needs were, he decided that the advisory was the wrong mechanism to meet their needs and so transformed it into the homework lab, where he taught the skills students needed to pass the college course; and at the conclusion of the semester, all of the UA students passed the college course. Formal opportunities for Barlowe to share his learnings with UA faculty led to a school policy to attach labs to demanding courses and to continue the homework lab for future UA-college collaborations. The lab attachment has increased the number of UA students who can enroll in and pass college courses.

When International's David Hirschy understood that students avoided taking physics because they thought they lacked the required math skills, he integrated math and physics by creating the Motion curriculum and interdisciplinary team. When Motion team teachers learned that students aimed for content mastery when they received a group rather than individual grade for their exhibitions, they institutionalized the policy across the team's classes. When they learned that their students were making private bargains with themselves to do less, marginal, or failing work in courses that required them to struggle, they initiated a fail-one-fail–all grading policy. This policy stipulated that students had to pass all the cluster courses in order to obtain credit for any one course. The policy produced higher course pass rates in difficult subject matter than any of the teachers individually had experienced when teaching solo. Eventually the whole school adopted the Motion team's strategy for increasing students' commitment to more ambitious learning (Ancess, 2000).

When Hodgson embarked upon their initiative to integrate mathematics and vocational education curriculum, Math and Shop teachers collaboratively designed a strategy based on Shop and Math teachers getting to know one another, learning about one another's work, and developing a professional relationship. Time was allocated for Math teachers to visit and teach in Shop classes and for Math and Shop teachers to engage in joint conversations and curriculum development. The classroom observations helped the teachers understand the nature of each other's content and what teaching and learning looked like in each other's classes. English chair MaryAn Scarbrough asserted, "Being in the shops helped [Math teachers] understand the language and experience of Shop classes–how they conceptualize their teaching."

Lutz explained how the initiative helped Shop teachers become more aware of the role that math played in their curriculum: "[The Math teachers] came down and observed what we do in the shops and literally told us math we were doing."

By working on shop projects alongside students in the Shop classes, in the second year of the initiative, and teaching the math that students needed as the need for it emerged, Math teachers deepened their understanding of how their students learned math. Derrickson understood why and how students could achieve success where previously they had failed:

> We could go slower–at their pace. Students who needed the
> extra help could get that. We would repeat these things over
> and over again. Kids who never had success in algebra
> before–because we were going at that slow rate–they really
> understood the concepts. They saw the application–they got
> it slow enough that they could understand it. They applied
> it. It addressed different types of learning, different learning
> styles.

The shop context enabled Math teachers to make new and useful meaning of their students' behavior and needs, which in turn directed them to make changes in their practice, resulting in increasing students' opportunities for success.

In each of the three schools, faculty also participate in external reviews of their work, so that they can apply outside perspectives to their judgments of their own work and to student performance. An external board of expert university professors and practitioners conducts reviews of the student performance assessment systems of UA and International. Outside experts sit on students' performance assessment committees in all three schools. Hodgson has enlisted a board of advisors that includes representatives from local businesses as well as educators to review the quality and relevance of its curriculum and instruction. Hodgson regularly surveys parents and students on their satisfaction with the school, and International and UA solicit student course evaluations. Feedback from their extended community informs faculty of what meaning others find in their work; influences changes in the schools' educational program; and provides opportunities for them to revisit their values, beliefs, commitments, and norms of practice.

CONCLUSION

Organizing teaching and learning so that students can make and find meaning in their school experiences raises questions as to whether and to what extent—as members of a particular school community and as members of a broader national community—we believe that an important purpose of school is to help youth to examine and make sense of their lives, their personal history, the history of their people, their personal assumptions and beliefs; and the beliefs, achievement, triumphs, tragedies, contradictions, myths, embarrassments, and evils of our nation and our world and invest in their own personal and our collective future. Do we trust our schools to prepare youth to take a close and hard look at our society? After close examination of our society, do we have faith that our youth will emerge capable of both understanding its worst moments and still believing in its values, principles, possibilities, and future, as well as their own possibilities and future in it? Do we want our schools to do more than prepare our youth to take their place in the workforce to support our economic structure? Do we want our schools to lecture students about the values and principles of our democracy or operationalize them so they can find meaning in them?

Hodgson, International, and the Urban Academy teach for meaning making because they consciously see and choose that as the role of school in our society and as an important component of their mission in educating youth. The schools' instructional approaches model the responsibility of meaning making—preparing students for a place in the economic structure of the nation but also the democratic structure as they teach habits of work but also the habits of mind and heart for life in a democracy: examining multiple perspectives on the basis of evidence, respecting diversity, and understanding the importance of human connection, commitment, community, and personal responsibility as teachers work to connect their practice to their students' learning needs, to the values and mission of their school community, to their personal beliefs and passions about the purposes of education in a democracy, to their own vitality and renewal as professionals. Students learn the complexity, struggle, and rewards of meaning making—they discover that they can transcend their own obstacles and boundaries and disappointments to achieve more than they had imagined possible.

Teaching and learning for making meaning can forge and strengthen connections between teachers and students and their school as an educational community. As teachers frame problems; develop and implement solutions; create courses and curriculum; and design instruction and assessments that reflect the convergence of their values, beliefs, interests and passions, their school's mission, and students' interests and needs, they imprint their personal stamp on their school. The presence of teachers' voices in the school culture and the schoolwide dissemination and application of the classroom practices they invent give palpable meaning to the teaching work of each school's particular teachers. The expectation for particularity in teachers' practice–that is, the idea that the schools expect teaching to be responsive to the particular students who are enrolled in them–conveys an authenticity to the work, and means that teachers can find meaning in the actual activities that comprise it, whether they are inventing a lab course, developing a social history approach, or teaching students math for a shop project. Their work is elicited by the needs and values of the school community. The norms of making teaching practice public, and in several instances (such as with the lab course) integrating it into the school culture, give teachers' work meaning on the broader school landscape. Individual teachers' contributions make a difference in their school and to their school. They are not cogs in a wheel or widgets, where one is indistinguishable from another.

Because teaching and learning are intended to be appealing and responsive to particular students, because curriculum and instruction are not designed for a "generic" student, and because they work off teachers' knowledge of students' interests and how they learn, students are able to find meaning in their school experiences. They are able to transcend self-imposed limitations. When pedagogy removes obstacles to achievement, whether it is biased, insensitive, or hurtful text or instructional approaches that constrain students' capacity to understand, students can find meaning that has eluded them in material. We see this in students' commentary on Warshawsky's Math class.

Teaching and learning for making meaning is incorporated into the schools' pedagogical mental models. Each school has created an elaborate instructional infrastructure that supports intellectual work and the possibilities of meaning making. That infrastructure includes the practice of revision, initiatives such as writing across the curriculum, the proactive, course-embedded, responsive interventions, and courses that teach students how to use a library, how to take notes from multiple sources of information, how to construct a bibliography, how to engage in a classroom discourse in ways that respect multiple perspectives, how to organize time for completing a task, ways of thinking and knowing in mathematics, and how to work in groups. These are the habits of mind and work and structures for thinking that make making meaning possible.

Teaching and learning for making meaning is important so that members of the school community stay personally connected to why they are doing what they are doing, in order to ensure that what they are doing is achieving ends that the school community values and desires, and in order to be able to honor the commitments expressed in their vision and mission. It is important for a school's credibility and accountability. If we want to teach students the value of finding meaning in work, then it is important for them and their teachers to work in an environment that encourages meaning making, where they bring their life, passion, interests, talents, and needs–their vitality–to their work and are not reduced to just "doing their time."

Pedagogy for meaning making demands vigilant commitment, as the present educational climate reminds us. The values of the current one-size-fits-all, high-stakes standardized tests accountability movement challenge and compete with the values that undergird teaching and learning for making meaning. The former is predicated on a distrust of schools and teachers and seeks unquestioned compliance, not commitment where the latter assumes trust and relies on commitment. Schools that aim to be communities of commitment have yet a new struggle to encounter, one that must be waged politically as well as educationally, where they must invent ways to prepare students for exams that may conflict with their mission and pedagogy. The New York schools, like others in a number of states across the country, have engaged in a legal battle with the State Education Department to secure the performance assessment accountability systems that protected their pedagogy and which was approved by a former administration. As the New York State Education Department has been criticized for censorship on its Regents English Language Arts exam, and as dropout rates in New York State are increasing, the legislature is holding hearings to reassess the new accountability.

Meanwhile, making meaning in the schools is not on hold. The new accountability system and the responses to it by students' and faculties' particular schools have become a legitimate topic of study for students and faculty across schools. There is a need to collaborate on strategies for strengthening teaching and learning for making meaning while developing test-preparation courses for the new exams . . . just in case.

CHAPTER 5

Possibilities for Schools as Communities of Commitment: What It Takes

Compliance was enough in [the old] days. . . . Today it's different. Compliance isn't enough. You need everyone's commitment because only with commitment will you get people to give 100%

—William Bridges, *Managing Transitions: Making the Most of Change*, p. 22

In this era of high standards for all, most of the students at the Urban Academy, International High School, and Hodgson would fit the profile of most likely casualties. Their histories, their demographics, and their ambivalence and resistance would seem to doom them to school failure. Yet they succeed beyond what their statistical profiles, school histories, and personal vulnerabilities would forecast, reminding us that in America, history and background need not be destiny, and schools and teachers can make a difference–that schools can be the "great equalizers," as Horace Mann anointed them. These schools remind us that you can still find public spaces where the American dream survives.

Although it is easy to marginalize the success of these schools–and many do, charging them with "creaming" students and selecting quality teachers, or being outliers and "boutiques" that can't be replicated or brought to scale because of the "special circumstances" of their conditions of operation, such as choosing their staff–these ways of thinking are more indicative of the normative expectation for public school failure than they are of any "special" conditions present at these schools. The problem lies in the failure of our collective imagination, which refuses to consider large-scale possibilities of successful breakthrough schools and which legitimizes only public school failure, thereby making it a self-fulfilling prophecy. What Hodgson, International, and Urban Academy show is that professional agency and particular internal conditions can elicit a set of student, teacher, and school behaviors that produce more desirable results. And even if anomalous conditions were responsible for the success of these schools, why would we not think of making–or want to make–the anomaly the norm? Why treat these schools' success as a deficit? Why repeatedly insist upon trying to make the unfixable model workable?

In this chapter, I review the internal conditions that elicit student and teacher commitment to make schools communities of commitment and external conditions necessary to safeguard schools such as these and bring them to scale.

INTERNAL CONDITIONS

In the preceding three chapters I described some of the organizational, relational, and instructional conditions that elicit student and teacher commitment, and which enable these schools to be high-performing communities of commitment. The human scale and organization of staff, students, time, space, and work and the structure of leadership and governance operationalize the schools to be educational communities; to enact their beliefs and vision of education; to promote students' intellectual, social, and emotional development; to elicit high-quality performance from faculty and students; and to support human connections, bonding, individual and collective responsibility, and continuous organizational improvement. Inclusive governance structures designed for broad participation, discourse, debate, diverse constituent voices, and knowledge sharing, building, and dissemination model responsible democratic citizenship and promote individuals' commitments to decisions that are made. Teachers have a strong sense of ownership over their individual and collective work. Opportunities for teachers to collaborate enable them to convert tacit knowledge into explicit knowledge, apply it to their work, and develop standards of professional practice that translate into the equitable dissemination of effective pedagogy to all students. Leaders are strong and distinctive; yet leadership is distributed across the staff so that all share authority and responsibility for the school community and school and student outcomes. While teacher authority and autonomy are respected, faculty understands the relationship between the interdependency of individuals and the viability of the school as a whole community. Their understanding supports policies and practices that balance and blend the individual and the common good. Teachers take on diffuse roles. Student self-expression is balanced by norms of interpersonal respect, such as Urban Academy's "no personal attacks" rule. Teachers' interests serve rather than compete with student and school: thematic courses for International's interdisciplinary teams embody teachers' interests and meet state requirements for student graduation; the design for Hodgson's academic and vocational integration builds on the teachers and students' strengths and successful school mechanisms.

Each of the schools has a system for obtaining external feedback on the quality of its program and student outcomes, which it combines along with internally derived feedback to determine the changes needed for improvement. This self-initiated pattern of continuous change for continuous improvement underscores the schools' trustworthiness and capacity for self-governance and self-regulation as well as their commitment to the quality achievement of their goals. The schools continuously reinvent themselves within the context of their mission and vision and make their success a self-fulfilling prophecy. It isn't that these schools are "boutiques" or have special teachers or students; rather, they are organized so that *failure is a very difficult option for students to choose.* This systems approach (Senge, 1990) promotes equitable distribution of successful practice as well as instructional and social cohesion, so that as communities the three schools can more powerfully, pervasively, and effectively achieve their mission to produce student success than would be possible if they were more typically organized as disconnected collections of individual teachers or departments that act independently in isolation.

Close, caring, and intense relationships between teachers and students, and among faculty who share students, are the central, most powerful driving force of the schools. These relationships teach students that they matter and that their learning matters. Relationships create the trusting bonds that catalyze the changes in students' performance. Similarly, opportunities for collegial collaboration and conversation and formal and informal faculty relationships generate and disseminate new knowledge, ignite change, and build the commitments that drive change in classroom and schoolwide practice. The organization of the schools creates the possibility for belonging, for the kind of interpersonal engagement that facilitates these intense, caring relationships—easy access, opportunities for serendipitous and intentional attachments, watchfulness over student work and behavior, expectations for teachers to know students well as learners and individuals, teacher push, shared beliefs and goals, and faculty collaboration and dialogue. The value placed on relationships as both a change-inducing and stabilizing strategy, and the nature and the structure of relationships possible in these schools enable teachers and students to effectively negotiate tensions which, in more traditionally organized schools, constitute obstacles to achievement. Student resistance and ambivalence, often regarded as pathological willfulness, is normalized in the three schools and coupled with teacher persistence. The schools do not make the resolution or elimination of students' resistance or ambivalence a precondition for learning or support. Instead, the schools facilitate students' development of intense relationships and strong attachments to their teachers, who can negotiate and renegotiate students' ambivalence and build the students' affiliation with their school's values and goals that is necessary for students to meet their learning demands. As a result, students have multiple opportunities to transcend powerful obstacles to achievement and success, as Stanley did at Hodgson.

The trust generated by students' relationships with their teachers enables students to persevere despite their resistance and ambivalence toward their school's demands for achievement. The results are higher rates of student success and personal payoffs, such as a greater sense of self-confidence, a more in-depth understanding of learning and of themselves as learners, increased skills and knowledge, and new possibilities for their future.

Because the schools' professional culture celebrates teacher persistence in response to student resistance and anoints it with status, teachers are systemically encouraged and supported to negotiate and renegotiate students' ambivalence, as Lutz did with Stanley. The schools' norm of teacher persistence supports teachers' commitment to eliciting—to teasing out—student achievement and becomes a standard of professional practice and an integral part of student success.

The social capital produced by relationships contributes to making the school a strong, cohesive, and effective community of commitment, one that provides sufficient energy, support, and benefits to faculty and students to do what is necessary to achieve their school's vision and mission and to make their personal investments in it worthwhile. Relentless teacher persistence can be frustrating, exhausting, and painful. Taken on by teachers in isolation, it is unsustainable. However, in the context of collegial relationships that offer encouragement, teachers persist, as illustrated by Lutz's commitment to what is known at UA as "nudge and nag, punch and stroke" pedagogy. International's teachers persist in negotiating student ambivalence around collaborative learning and social responsibility. Collegial relationships, professionalism, intellectual stimulation, personal satisfaction, validation, and greater productivity—such as teachers' investment in Hodgson's math integration initiative—characterize the teacher culture across the schools. The capacity of relationships to generate social capital fortifies the schools as communities that can produce powerful results in the lives of their members.

The schools view students not as generic abstractions, but rather as individuals whose unique experiences demand respect and influence decisions. UA's Ann Cook says students "know they are listened to." Students have a voice—in school governance, in relationships, in instruction, in the courses they take, in the projects and assignments within courses, and in their life as lived in school. In multiple ways the schools inform their students that they want them to make an investment in their own education and that they want them to choose to learn.

Choice, responsive pedagogy focused on making meaning, the value of student and teacher voice, and an infrastructure of support to monitor student progress and prevent failure all elicit commitment from teachers and students. These features that characterize the schools' instructional component send the message that teachers and students matter, that teachers' pedagogy and students' learning matter, and that individuals and the school intend and have the capacity to make a difference. Teachers are trusted decision makers whose authority, judgments, and opinions are respected and count. Teachers choose the colleagues with whom they want to team up. They choose and design the courses they teach and the curricular organization. Their individual interests, passions, and expertise are valuable resources in their design of unique interdisciplinary as well as discipline-based courses and curriculum on topics that embody those interests as well as students' interests, backgrounds, histories, learning needs, and state and local graduation requirements.

The schools' commitment to the intellectual development of students as thinking individuals prepared to function productively in our democracy and to the development and expression of student voice is found in pedagogy that engages students in meaning making, as opposed to the more conventional passive reception of predigested, canned knowledge. Customized teaching, curriculum, and assessment respond to students' histories and strengths (not deficits) as learners and their experiences as individuals in the world, providing them with new entry points and access to the knowledge and skills that will serve them personally and as active citizens and that will be required for graduation. The structure of learning opportunities, as exemplified in Warshawsky's math classes, teaches students that there are multiple ways of learning and develops their confidence in their own approaches, even when they are untraditional or require more support than their peers.

Curriculum content–as in International's Social History Project, UA's courses such as "Novels: Getting to Like Them" or "Misfits in Literature," and Hodgson's vocational and academic integration–builds on students interests, experiences, and issues, yet is aligned to state standards. Assessments inform instruction and provide students with opportunities to show what they know and can do in multiple ways and to have confidence in their knowledge, especially when their achievement is not accurately measured by standardized tests.

Teaching and learning for making meaning prepares students for a range of intellectual challenges they will face in their future at postsecondary institutions, in jobs, and in society. Learning tasks demand hypothesizing, analysis, synthesis, knowledge production, listening with an open mind, questioning, evaluation, and judgment making. They support the struggle for understanding by requiring students to raise questions, consider multiple and conflicting perspectives from multiple sources of information, and challenge their peers' arguments. They support quality performance by providing opportunities for students to practice the skills for oral defenses–where students' understanding is assessed–and to revise their papers. In fact, the schools have a culture of revision where, guided by their teachers, students regularly rewrite papers to improve their quality.

A formal infrastructure of support guards against failure and provides even more opportunities for achievement, whether it is individual tutoring, homework labs, or library curriculum. In each of the schools, the sheer number of opportunities for students to achieve is testimony to the schools' commitment to their success. Student benefits include feelings of confidence and empowerment, a sense of agency about their own learning, self-knowledge and meta-cognitive capacity, improved performance, and more ambitious postgraduation aspirations.

While these schools may not be typical, to deny that they *can* be typical is an assertion of will to prevent them from being typical and a repudiation of the belief that environment can affect human behavior.

EXTERNAL CONDITIONS

If schools like Hodgson, International, and Urban Academy are rare, perhaps we need to examine the external conditions in which schools exist. Hodgson, International, and Urban Academy are communities of commitment by their own design. They are school- and practitioner-based reforms. They were neither initiated nor designed by state or local education agencies or external "experts." Nor are they replications of pre-established models. They are responses to practitioners' knowledge and understanding of the conditions and supports adolescents need in order to learn. They have sustained through the occasional advocacy, serendipitous goodwill, blind eye of authorities, or policy by exception (Darling-Hammond, Ancess, McGregor, & Zuckerman, 2000), but ultimately by the strength of their commitment to the powerful ideas and beliefs at their core and their own political capital. The Hodgson school community appealed to Delaware's New Castle Vocational District to pass an official resolution making the Senior Project a graduation requirement, thereby more powerfully rooting into the school culture those pedagogical practices aligned with it. Several times, International successfully fought the New York State Education Department for approval of its innovative approach to English language learning. Urban Academy and International, along with a consortium of schools, applied for and were granted a waiver by the New York State Education Department to graduate students by an externally validated system of performance assessment in lieu of state Regents exams.

New York City Board of Education central office high school officials such as Sylvia Ballatt, John Ferrandino, and Stephen Phillips established risk-seeking environments that coupled school-based trust and accountability to produce and protect schools like Urban Academy and International. Ballatt encouraged and supported practitioners to imagine and create innovative schools for underserved youth. Phillips brokered conflicts between the schools and the bureaucracy. Ferrandino protected site-based autonomy and decision-making by encouraging school-based problem solving while simultaneously watching organizational and student outcomes. Each generated good public relations by broadcasting school successes among colleagues and system leaders. Early on, key Board of Education leaders knew about the schools' achievements. System insiders navigated the schools through the New York City Byzantine maze of school bureaucracy.

While advocacy by school system officials and policy by exception can be sufficient short-term strategies to protect the commitments of schools such as these three, for the long term such schools are vulnerable to bureaucratic rigidity, the shifting winds of politics that care not at all about outcomes or track records, unpredictable budgets, and fickle educational philosophies that challenge school-based commitments and practitioner commitment-making. The volatility of the educational landscape calls for central offices to develop the kind of conditions and infrastructure that sustainability and scaling up such models require, and to institutionalize those conditions provided by the short-term advocacy and policy variances described above. Even where there is continuity in district leadership and policy, as there has been for the last 10 years in Del Castle County, in order to root what works, state and local education agencies need to transform their traditions, norms, and habits of policy discontinuity, crisis management, role-based authority, distrust, linear power relations, and intolerance for difference.

Policy Discontinuity

In education tradition, policy continuity is an anomaly. Policy continuity need have no relationship to policy effect. Instead, policy continuity is a function of politics. Because the political demand for leaders to make their mark encourages new leaders to arbitrarily reverse the policies, systemic supports, and commitments of their predecessors—regardless of their effectiveness or popularity—policy discontinuity becomes inevitable (Ancess & Ort, 1999). Because new administrations are under no obligation to honor the commitments made to schools by their predecessors, no innovation, no matter how successful, is secure. Any state or local administration can and does supercede the decisions of preceding administrations without consideration of the consequences to schools, practitioners, students, parents, and their own credibility.

This fickle organizational behavior can and does challenge the operation of school commitments and raises questions of system-level accountability to parents and students as well as to the educators who make commitments to particular educational reforms. It takes so many years to bring reforms to maturity and to achieve their promise that, unless they are protected from the shifting winds of education politics, critical opportunities for sustaining reform and commitments–particularly those that increase the chances of success for under-served youngsters about whom the public is ambivalent supporting–will be squandered.

This tradition of policy discontinuity undermines practitioner commitment and schools' efforts to establish professional standards of practice, pedagogical expertise, and a culture of accountability that is defined by the proliferation of effective practice and the elimination of harmful practice (Darling-Hammond & Snyder, 1992). Such undermining is evident in the efforts of the New York State Education Department to arbitrarily reverse its former commissioner's policy supporting valid, locally developed high school graduation assessment systems such as the one designed by UA, International, and a consortium of 40 schools across the state. The public, governors, and legislatures need to hold education bureaucracies accountable for safeguarding from arbitrary change those programs and schools that have demonstrated effectiveness. Otherwise, schools such as UA, International, and Hodgson are indeed in danger of being transitory occurrences.

Crisis Management

The long-term survival and proliferation of schools that are communities of commitment ultimately requires school systems to develop new habits of managing change so that they can meet the challenge of sustaining and growing exemplary models. Particularly in times of crisis, when nontraditional schools are most vulnerable, school systems need new habits of managing change that do not sacrifice their exemplary programs. Conventionally, school systems manage crisis by shifting the location of their problem. They transfer their crisis at the central office to the school, where the school then has the responsibility of resolving it. For example, if a community experiences an infusion of new students, districts overcrowd schools regardless of the effect on the school's safety, stability, instruction, or capacity for intervention and student support. Since problems such as fluctuation in population recur, and overcrowding schools diminishes educational outcomes, school systems should develop a set of plans that would not sacrifice functioning schools and could be applied when the problem arises. When districts place student access in competition with the human-scale conditions essential to students' achievement of high standards, they undermine the success of schools such as UA, International, and Hodgson. Strategic and contingency planning and other strategies for managing unpredictable yet recurring issues, such as population increases, can safeguard against the casualties of competing priorities.

Role-Based Authority, Linear Power Relations, and Distrust of Schools

Competency-based authority (Elmore, 2000) rather than role-based authority, trust rather than distrust of schools, negotiated power relations rather than one-way, linear power relations, "top-down support for bottom-up reform," and reciprocal accountability between schools and their regulatory agencies can support schools as communities of commitment. Del Castle School District supported innovative, teacher-created curriculum models such as Hodgson's interdisciplinary "American Experience" History/Language Arts course. When the Del Castle School District allocated funds for math integration, key school system leaders did not mandate an implementation plan; rather, they legitimated Hodgson's authority to control its own development by trusting the school to design a competent approach consistent with its culture and targeted to improving student outcomes.

When a district can support flexibility, risk-taking, and site-based autonomy and accountability, it can produce schools that are communities of commitment. Former executive director of New York City's high schools, John Ferrandino, explains:

> You give good people their lead, trust them, give them flexibility, and do not interfere. But you watch their data. You let them do what they need to do. You need to do this in an urban setting to succeed with every kid: get good people and let them do their thing.

He and others with and before him created an environment hospitable to the kinds of reform that International and Urban Academy produced.

The sense of agency these schools possess and assert also alters power relations (as well as their relationship) with their local and state bureaucracies. They do not withdraw from conflict or clashes in policy, but engage officials in dialogue and debate about what is best, what is possible, and what is necessary in order to produce a quality education for their students. They take principled stands, which sometimes irritate their school systems or create political inconvenience. They seek external support by joining local and national networks and forming relationships with parents, local politicians, and business and community leaders. Although sometimes discouraged, they refuse to be defeated. When they lose a round, they return at another time or devise another strategy. In some instances their refusal to compromise on their commitments has been met with sanctions. Still, they endure. Their defiant insistence to educate their students in schools that demonstrate their commitments sustains them.

Tolerance for Difference

Schools that are communities of commitment require school systems to value diversity and to relinquish the mistaken belief that equity is achieved by uniformity. The practice of differentiation allows schools to be responsive to the concerns of their local population and to the learning needs of their students, to support those pedagogical practices that work most effectively to secure student achievement. Policies such as New York City's school-based option—which permits schools to bypass particular work conditions when they obtain agreement from 55% of teachers—exemplify the kind of variation needed. Mandates for uniformity can undermine local innovation and coerce compliance with practices and policies that conflict with site-based educators' values, knowledge, experience, and judgments about what achieves the standards they set. They undermine teachers' accountability for finding the practice that works best with their particular students. They undermine school community responsibility.

SCALING UP

Scaling up schools that are communities of commitment presents complex challenges to school systems because the values and norms by which school systems operate are essentially not compatible with the values and norms of communities of commitment. Being bureaucracies, school systems seek compliance, uniformity, predictability, and control. While commitment may be nice or tolerable in a few schools, it is at best irrelevant and at worst an obstacle to the highly valued compliance. The continuous change and organic growth essential for the continuous improvement and accountability that characterize Hodgson, International, and UA exacerbate the bureaucracy's inherent distrust of schools and practitioners and threaten its sense of control and need for uniformity and predictability. The central office or state education department can't be sure what is going on in these schools at any given time. And they look different from year to year! Education bureaucracies see schools that are communities of commitment as trouble because they make demands, they raise questions, they take charge of their destiny, they change the structure of power relations with their district, and they upend the social order by giving the "bottom" kids access to the rewards that were once the exclusive privilege of the elite.

The destabilizing effect these kinds of schools can have on the bureaucracy makes even their success with students of no consequence to the school system. No wonder school system bureaucrats assert that these schools are boutiques that don't scale up. In the current culture of school bureaucracies, schools as communities of commitment can't scale up because the bureaucracies don't want them to scale up; they don't want a system of such schools, and even if they did, they would have to reculture and reorganize themselves because as is, they do not have the capacity to bring them to scale.

Small efforts to scale up schools that are communities of commitment have succeeded where those educators who created and implemented the originals have guided others in the creation of similar schools and have raised funds and negotiated with the school system to create them. Supported by private and Board of Education funding, Nadelstern has mentored the development of three new-generation schools based on the principles of International. In two cases the principals of the new-generation schools were former faculty members at the "mother" school, and the principal of the third school interned with Nadelstern. International faculty such as David Hirschy collaborated with faculty at the new-generation schools to develop curriculum incorporating the principles and lessons of pedagogy learned and practiced at the "mother" school. Although the three new-generation schools embrace the core principles of the original, they frequently customize their implementation so that they are operationalized in response to their context. Their fidelity is more to the educational principles of the original International than to its structures.

Another effort to scale up schools that are communities of commitment occurred in the early 1990s when Deborah Meier and Marsha Shelton Brevot secured private funding and school system support to develop several schools committed to the principles of the Coalition of Essential Schools and based on the beliefs and designs of Central Park East Secondary School (CPESS), International, and Urban Academy. (See Darling-Hammond, Ancess, McGregor, & Zuckerman, 2000; and Darling-Hammond, Ancess, & Ort-Wichterle, 2002 for studies on the Coalition Campus Schools.) In most instances, the initial success of these new-generation schools sustains for the tenure of the founding leader. If the school community can wield enough political clout to secure a successor who is committed to the school's values and principles and is capable of enacting them, then the school can sustain longer. However, when founding principals leave, too often the school system appoints new leaders without regard to their knowledge of or commitment to the school's commitments. Not surprisingly, within 2 years staff all but completely turn over and the culture dissolves.

In a school system that does not acknowledge or value diversity or lacks the will and capacity to support schools organized to be communities rather than bureaucracies, any cog will do, and schools that are communities of commitment, that require and rely on a match, are systemically undermined. Although Meier proposed the creation of a "learning zone" to protect the schools from an undermining regulatory environment and also hold them accountable through a process of peer and external review, the school system rejected the plan. In the absence of safeguards, the schools have experienced the erosion of prior state and city agreements essential to the sustainability of their core features, such as graduation by performance assessments and small school size.

Does this mean that schools seeking to be communities of commitment are doomed? No. What it means is that innovation cannot endure without core change in state and local education regulatory agencies. If school systems are major obstacles to the sustainability of new educational models, how likely are they to support going to scale? How then can successful innovations such as schools that are communities of commitment be brought to scale?

The Twin Challenges of Scale

Successful scale up of schools that are communities of commitment requires reform of the central office and of schools. School system central offices need to reculture and reorganize so that they can support the systemic development and maintenance of schools that are communities of commitment. By reculturing, I mean transforming the values and assumptions upon which central offices function and their ways of doing business as well as reconceptualizing the role and function of the central office in the areas of monitoring, professional development, accountability, authority, power relations with schools, standardization, and scaling up reform.

The function of monitoring must make way for capacity building and support. Conceptions of accountability must change from compliance to collective responsibility for student outcomes and implementation of pedagogy that produces desired outcomes. Processes need to be developed for enacting reciprocal accountability between schools and their districts so that schools have a voice in policy making and districts can be responsible for the outcomes their policies produce. Funding and decision making for professional development must shift from districts to schools, and incentives must be provided for schools to design their own professional development that builds on their practices and that demonstrates evidence of achieving their goals. Conceptions of authority must change from being role-based to being competency-based, and power relations must shift away from hierarchy, rigidity, and mandates to make room for dialogue, flexibility, and negotiation.

The belief that uniformity produces equity must yield to the understanding that diverse contexts require diverse responses. Subsequently, the vision for standardization must surrender to a vision for a differentiated system whereby districts support local variation and accord autonomy to schools based upon their *progress* in the achievement of agreed upon goals. Some goals may be common across schools and some may be customized. The nature and rate of progress must consider the complexity of the change required. Just as one-size pedagogy does not fit all students or produce uniformly high standards, a one-size system does not fit all schools or make them high-performance organizations.

Conceptions about scaling up must also change from replicating the structure of successful innovations to replicating the conditions that produced them. Traditionally, school systems try to scale up successful models by replicating their organization and structures without realizing that structure is a strategy developed in response to a need to achieve particular goals developed in a particular context and culture. Schools that are encouraged and have the capacity to be responsive to their students, community, and mission will produce their own effective structures just as Hodgson, International, and UA produced unique structures for personalization. In order for large numbers of schools to develop the capacity for such responsiveness, they need a regulatory environment that values, supports, is hospitable to, and rewards local responsiveness and, consequently, variation.

The conditions of development for Hodgson, International, and UA were particular. Critical local and state leaders altered enough regulations, inhospitable conditions, and policies to facilitate their growth. To scale up schools such as these, local and state education agencies need to make those hospitable conditions available on a broader scale. They need to create the conditions that will yield the type of schools they want to "replicate," support their development, and establish a set of policies that will sustain these schools.

Coupled with reculturing, central offices need to reorganize so that they can implement the new values, beliefs, and mission. By reorganizing the central office, I mean developing structures, mechanisms, and processes that customize and personalize relations with schools; that generate district personnel's responsiveness to schools and encourage and reward their investment in the success, rather than the failure, of innovations; that seek feedback from schools for the purposes of fine tuning central office operations; and that facilitate the dissemination of effective local practice. In short, central offices need to communicate their support for the success of the schools.

The second challenge of scaling up schools that are communities of commitment rests within the schools themselves. Schools must reconceptualize faculty roles and responsibilities, organizational norms, pedagogy, accountability, professional development, and work arrangements such as the use of time. Although new efforts can borrow from existing models, ultimately they must develop the value and capacity to engage in a process of intentional, organic growth whereby they can convert their tacit knowledge into explicit knowledge, which they then use to drive change. Opportunities for faculty collaboration as well as the commitment to and skills for effective collaboration enabled Hodgson, International, and UA to design strategies to invent and reinvent themselves in response to both the demands of students' emergent needs and to new knowledge emanating from their practice. While new initiatives can draw on successful organizational, relational, and pedagogical structures of effective schools that are communities of commitment, they will have little chance of replicating their benefits and results unless the new initiatives are willing to learn first hand what those structures mean and how they take meaning in their particular school. Replication of results requires schools to have the capacity and agency to invent, reinvent, and change themselves.

When only structural change occurs, as when schools are "broken down" into smaller versions of their bigger selves, assumptions about students remain unchanged. Pedagogy remains unchanged. Relationships are not used to leverage student progress and achievement. Teachers continue to teach in isolation in test-prep-accountability environments. The cohesion that yields higher levels of achievement eludes the new entity. Structural change changes structure, not substance.

Schools need to make sense out of what is going on inside them—in their classrooms, in their halls, in their students hearts and minds, and in their teachers' imaginations—so that they can develop strategies that make sense in terms of what they want to achieve. They also need resources to engage in this self-reflective process. Opportunities that support this kind of learning, analysis, and growth include faculty residencies at schools that engage in these practices as well as the networking of like-minded schools of varying maturity to facilitate cross-school learning as well as principal and teacher learning. New York City has rewarded schools for mentoring other schools in need. Foundations such as Goldman Sachs have supported such voluntary networks of like-minded schools. The Bill and Melinda Gates small school grantees have participated in residencies at International and Urban Academy.

However, even the will and capacity of schools to become communities of commitment will not be sufficient for extensive scale up. State and local education agencies will have to change their culture of coercive compliance and conformity. Creating more schools like Hodgson, International, and the Urban Academy will require a hunger to change the status quo.

CONCLUSION

The schools we create and support reflect the commitment we have to our children, our children's future, and our future as a nation. At the creation of our nation, Thomas Jefferson envisioned public education as the vehicle for preserving democracy and safeguarding against tyranny. Public education could produce an "intelligence populace and a popular intelligence" (Darling-Hammond & Ancess, 1996, p. 153) whereby individuals would be prepared to engage fully in the democratic deliberation necessary for self-rule. The current education landscape reflects our nation's ambivalence toward this role for public education. Our schools provide compelling evidence that we care about some children more than we care about others and still others we care about little or not at all. Like it or not, the inequitable distribution of education that prepares future citizens for full participation in our democracy has consequences to our society. To be careless in the education for our future is to be careless with our democracy. While the national education discourse is robust about the relationship between schools and our economy and our global economic pre-eminence, where is it on the relationship between schools and our democracy, social justice, and equity? The "good life" in the American dream is more than an economic fantasy. And how secure can we be in the good life for ourselves if access to the opportunities for it are systematically denied to segments of our population?

Schools such as Hodgson, International, and Urban Academy are thoughtful and deliberate in their mission for the future of their students as citizens and as individuals. As communities of commitment, these schools have a particular vision of our nation and of the role their efforts at education can play to prepare their students for full participation in it. As schools that make commitments and take risks to keep commitments and each day live their commitments, Hodgson, International, and Urban Academy teach their students important lessons about the principles, the price, and the value of our democracy. These are lessons we all need to take to heart.

Appendix

EXHIBIT 1

URBAN ACADEMY SCHEDULE

MONDAY	TUESDAY	WEDNESDAY
8:30–9:30 AM　　**A** Algebra 2 Animal Behavior Fitness Geometry A Math Lab O Brother! O Sister! Sketch Book Art *9:30–9:40 BREAK* **9:40–10:45 AM**　　**B** American History Colonial Literature Constitutional Law Gym Power–*The Generation of Electricity* Raising Ourselves **10:45–11:45 AM**　　**C** Organizational Tutorial *Avram, Barry, Cathy, Dickson, Gail, Marcela, Nancy, Rachel B., Rachel W., Roy, Terri G., Terry W.* **11:45–12:45 LUNCH** **12:45–1:45 PM**　　**D** Homework Lab for Swing Dance Ethics Horticulture, Introduction Just Say No Little Big Books Looking for an Argument? Lost in Transition Science Projects Trumpet Yearbook *1:45–1:55 BREAK* **1:55–3:00 PM**　　**E** Public Art Installations Jazz The Top Ten Greatest Films of All Time Trigonometry E Urban Studies **3:10–5:10 PM** Improv Club Homework Lab (3:10–4:30) Math (3:15–4:30)	**8:30–10:15 AM**　　**F** Advanced Photography Basic Repair and Maintenance Bugs Ceramics Computer Programming Drug Wars Geometry F Novels Who is Hero? *9:25–9:35 BREAK* **10:15–11:10 AM**　　**D** Homework Lab for: Just Say No, Trumpet, Yearbook Horticulture, Introduction Little Big Books Looking for an Argument? Lost in Transition Montana Planners Science Projects Swing Dance **11:10–12:00 PM**　　**G** Full Group or Conversations **12:00–1:00 LUNCH** **1:00–3:00 PM**　　**H** Homework Lab for Weight Room (First half of H) About Men and Women Advanced Playwriting Workshop Boxing Horticulture, Advanced Social Documentary Photography Trigonometry H Weight Room Working in a Series *Yanqui Si?/Yanqui No?* *1:55–2:05 BREAK* **3:10–5:10 PM** Homework Lab (3:10–4:30) Math (3:15–4:30) Social Doc Photo Lab	**8:30–9:30 AM**　　**A** Algebra 2 Animal Behavior Fitness Geometry A Math Lab O Brother! O Sister! Sketch Book Art **9:30–10:30 AM**　　**B** American History Colonial Literature Constitutional Law Gym Power–*The Generation of Electricity* Raising Ourselves *10:30–10:40 BREAK* **10:40–11:30 AM**　　**C** Organizational Tutorial *Avram, Barry, Cathy, Dickson, Gail, Marcela, Nancy, Rachel B., Rachel W., Roy, Terri G., Terry W.* Student Committee (Wed. Only) **11:30–12:15 LUNCH** **12:15–3:00 PM**　　**I** Community Service

THURSDAY	FRIDAY	
8:30–10:15 AM　　　**F**	**8:30–9:40 AM**　　　**A**	**First Steps Schedule:**
Homework Lab for: Drug Wars, Novels (First half of F)	Algebra 2 Animal Behavior	**12:00–1:00**
Advanced Photography	Fitness	Monday: Cathy
Basic Repair and Maintenance	Geometry A	Tuesday: Sasha
Bugs	Math Lab	Wednesday: Rachel B./Gail
Ceramics	O Brother! O Sister!	Thursday: Rachel W.
Computer Programming	Sketch Book Art	Friday: Phyllis
Drug Wars		
Geometry F	*9:40–9:50 BREAK*	
Novels		
Who is hero?	**9:50–11:00 AM**　　　**B**	
	American History	
9:20–9:30 BREAK	Colonial Literature	**Lang Schedule**
	Constitutional Law	Jennifer & Lee　　*T, Th 9–10:40*
10:15–11:15 PM　　　**D**	Gym	Alina & Vance　　*T, Th 4–5:40*
Ethics	Power–*The Generation of Electricity*	Luke & Zack　　*T, Th 4–5:40*
Horticulture, Introduction		
Just Say No	Raising Ourselves	
Little Big Books		
Looking for an Argument?	**11:00–12:00 LUNCH and BOXING**	
Lost in Transition		
Science Projects		
Swing Dance	**12:00–1:50 PM**　　　**H**	**Hunter Schedule**
Trumpet Yearbook	About Men and Women	Julian　　　　M, Th 1:10–3:40
	Advanced Playwriting Workshop	Natalia　　　T, Th 3:10–5:00
11:15–12:15 LUNCH	Boxing	Richard M.　　M, Th 4:10–5:25
	Horticulture, Advanced	Wanda　　　　M, Th 2:45–4:00
12:15–3:00 PM　　　**E**	Social Documentary Photography	
Public Art	Trigonometry H	
Installations	Weight Room	
Jazz	Working in a Series	
The Top Ten Greatest Films of All Time	*Yanqui Si?/Yanqui No?*	**NYU Schedule**
Trigonometry E	Homework Lab for Weight Room (Second Half of H)	Kola　　　　　　T 2:00
Urban Studies		
	1:00–1:10 BREAK	
3:10–4:30 PM		
Homework Lab (3:10–4:30)	**1:50–3:00 PM**　　　**E**	
Public Art Lab	Homework Lab for Trigonometry E	**Internships**
	Installations	Richard: Wednesday
	Jazz	Torri: PM, Monday–Friday
	Public Art	
	The Top Ten Greatest Films of All Time	
	Urban Studies	

EXHIBIT 2

PAUL M. HODGSON
VOCATIONAL–TECHNICAL HIGH SCHOOL
1998–99 STEERING COMMITTEE GOALS

I. STAFF DEVELOPMENT

1. By November 1998, implement a training plan to support teamwork, decision-making and consensus-building for all Steering Committee members.

2. By the end of the first marking period, plan and conduct an in-service day program to revisit the mission statement, which will include members of the total school community.

II. READING INITIATIVE

During the first marking period, a faculty committee will be formed to identify and aid in implementing strategies to improve learning and reading comprehension across the curriculum.

III. INSTRUCTION

During the 1998–99 school year, develop and implement a series of staff development opportunities that promote innovative instructional practice.

IV. COMMUNICATION

1. To establish a consistent schoolwide communication process of relaying ideas and information through scheduled conversations, and a suggestion box by the beginning of October 1998. (The communication goals are not complete as of 8/12/98.)

2. By December 1, 1998, poll the faculty, by survey, to evaluate our level of performance on 25% of the Steering Committee goals.

V. INTEGRATION

To foster integration of vocational and academic education through:

- Organizing teams to visit students on worksite   Establishing list of volunteers to participate in classroom visitations (October 1998)
- Scheduling two 30-minute share-a-thons (early 1st mp) (early 3rd mp)
- Annual theme approach–doesn't need to be a "thing." Example: volunteerism (all year)

EXHIBIT 3
INTERNATIONAL CURRICULUM

THE AMERICAN DILEMMA

If American culture is drawn from a rich tapestry of native and immigrant subcultures, historical events and decisions and shared legends of greatness, the rhythm of culture is as often fraught with conflict as it is characterized by consensus. Consensus is the culture we agree to and conflict is the necessary ingredient that moves it forward.

Essential Question:

What are the social conflicts reflected in American Literature? How are they resolved?

The Conflict and Resolution in America class will examine these issues through the study of literature. Your research will culminate in the production of a creative portfolio. This will demonstrate what you've discovered about your "vision of America."

Influences on American Culture

Racism, love, aging, death, democracy, pragmatism, individualism, conformity, violence, resistance, civil disobedience, fear/horror, psychology, money, immigration, assimilation, class struggle, Native Americans, slavery, generation gap, the West, the Civil War, gender, sexual orientation, the family, TV.

Themes and Materials in Literature

- Benjamin Franklin–time, money (utilitarianism/pragmatism)
- Tom Paine, Langston Hughes, Walt Whitman, Abigail Adams–democracy
- Fredrick Douglass, Charles Chestnutt, Malcolm X, Richard Wright, Martin Luther King, Jr.–oppression, racism, slavery, literacy, civil disobedience
- Nathaniel Hawthorne–youth and aging (*Dr. Hedigger's Experiment*)
- Edgar Allan Poe–horror and psychology (*The Pit and the Pendulum*)
- Mark Twain–social satire, writing in the vernacular (language of the common man: *Huckleberry Finn*)
- Sojourner Truth–women's rights (*Ain't I a Woman?*)
- Howard Fast–generation gap, independence (*April Morning*)
- Bintel Brief, Jesus Colon–immigration, assimilation (letters to the *Jewish Daily Forward*, *A Puerto Rican in New York*)

- Jack London–class struggle, love (*South of the Slot*)
- Ambrose Bierce, Louisa May Alcott–the Civil War (*Horseman in the Sky, Civil War Nurse*)
- Lorraine Hansberry–the family (*Raisin in the Sun*)
- Art Buchwald–TV (*The Shock of Recognition*)
- Stephen Crane–the West (*The Bride Comes to Yellow Sky*)

INTERDISCIPLINARY CONCEPTS
ESSENTIAL QUESTIONS

In our own lives, in our communities, and in our nation, we can find many examples of conflict. Sometimes we are able to resolve these conflicts and move on. Sometimes these conflicts reappear in the same or in new ways. One thing we know for sure: conflict is a part of life. However, even though we know this, many questions remain:

- What would life be like without conflict?
- Where do conflicts come from in our own lives?
- What happens when we ignore our conflicts?
- How have people attempted to resolve conflicts in America's past? Who won? Who lost?
- What conflicts from the past are still with us today?
- How would you attempt to resolve them for yourself? For this country?
- What role does mathematics play in solving conflict?
- How can conflicts be expressed and resolved in art?

At the end of this cycle, we will ask you to prepare a portfolio. These are the questions we will study this cycle in art, math, personal, and career development and history. These are the questions to which you must develop your own answers. These are the questions that you will address in your portfolio. Based on your answers, we will know what you have learned.

CONFLICT AND RESOLUTION
INTERDISCIPLINARY CURRICULUM

History

How do we know what the conflicts are, present and past? If we know by analyzing reality, how do we know reality?

Observation, Knowledge, Deduction

This is one method that reveals points of conflict and points of resolution. It also helps us to know what we know and what we still want to know (our questions for further research).

> *Activities:*
>
> 1. Use observation, knowledge, deduction chart to analyze visual images
> 2. What is an American?
> 3. Langston Hughes/*New Colossus*
> 4. Current Events
> 5. Journal writing: Mosaic vs. Melting Pot (Immig)
> 6. ASHP, *Heaven Will Protect the Working* Girl video
> 7. Tenement Museum/University Settlement
> 8. Archeology Project (study of historical conflicts/what were the attempts to resolve them/who won and who lost/what conflicts still remain today?)

PCD

How do we know what our personal conflicts are? If we know by examining the reality of our lives, what is that reality? What role does conflict play in our personal development?

Observation, Knowledge, Deduction

We will study ourselves in a systematic way using different means of data collection. We will look at what we know through the facts of our lives, we will observe our feelings and our dreams, and through all this we will be making deductions about who we are and what dream/career aspirations we have for the future. As part of our deductions, we will make internship selections.

1. Who am I activity and personal journal writing
2. Values inventory/April Morning
3. Resume writing
4. Career directory
5. Self-esteem game
6. Obituary tombstone
7. Obstacles in life
8. *Wall Street* video

Math

What role does math play in our lives? In life we have to make many important decisions. How do we know if we're making the right decisions? One way we can test it is by using mathematics. By learning different mathematical methods for solving conflicts/problems, we can learn tools for systematic, logical thinking.

Observation, Knowledge, Deduction

Activities:

1. Observations to graphs
2. Knowledge about correlation
3. Theory of correlation and prediction
4. Regression and line of best fit
5. Current Events—analyzing statistics
6. Introduction to hypothesis testing

EXHIBIT 4
URBAN ACADEMY COURSE CATALOG
SPRING

About Men and Women, The Sequel (Gail)

How important are family relationships when it comes to choosing a partner? Why are you attracted to one person but not another? How do you choose your friends? Partners? What are the responsibilities of a friend? Romantic partner? How do those you love know they are loved? What is love, anyway?

We will explore these questions and more through readings, discussion, interview, and writing. Be prepared to reflect and discuss.

Requirement: You passed About Men and Women or have permission from Gail.

Advanced Genetics Seminar (Barry)

This course is a continuation of Genetics 1. In Advanced Genetics, we will study genetics concepts in more depth (e.g., complex traits like skin color and height, linkage, and lethal genes). Through extensive readings, we will research to what extent genes control different aspects of our behavior (e.g., violence, alcoholism, mental illness, and intelligence). Several papers (of varying lengths) will be required.

Each student will continue the genetics project involving Drosophila (fruit flies) that was begun last semester. Satisfactory completion of this project can fulfill the student's science proficiency.

This class is open only to students who have completed Genetics 1.

Advanced Journalism: Strange Brew (Rachel W. and Becky)

Do you love to write? Like to work with other students? Have ideas about how our newspaper can serve and interest the Urban community?

In this course a small team of students will work together to write and publish *Strange Brew*. Together, students will decide what topics should be covered, workshop articles, and publish the paper. Students will focus on improving their own writing and putting together the school newspaper.

Prerequisite: Urban Academy writing course or consent of Rachel W. or Becky.

Advanced Photography (Roy)

In this class, students with more than a basic knowledge of the camera and darkroom processes can further their exploration into the medium. Amongst various weekly projects and assignments, the class will create imagery and discuss what makes it visually important. Projects will include advanced photo techniques and experimentation with alternative ways of making photographic imagery. We will also be visiting various museums and galleries around the city that concentrate on displaying photographic images. A final portfolio of class work will be required.

Students will be responsible for creating and maintaining displays in the school corridor throughout the semester.

Advanced Playwriting Workshop (Rachel W.)

This once-a-week workshop, open only to students who took the workshop last semester, gives students a chance to finish their plays and/or start new dramatic work. Some time will be set aside for writing, but mostly we'll use it to read and critique each other's drafts. Chris will be joining us for some of the meetings.

Algebra 2 (Terry)

Material: This class is a continuation of Algebra 1 and will cover: Distributive Law, factoring, 2 by 2 equations, coordinate geometry, exponents and roots, nth terms, the quadratic formula, patterns, symbolic equations, and graphing.

Methods: Puzzles and playing games. You will work mainly in small groups. Your job is to "figure out and explain." There will be regular homework, closed-book quizzes, and two open-book tests.

American History (Avram)

"It's a free country" is a saying that almost every American is familiar with. It is an expression rooted in the belief that our political system, which was established over 200 years ago, makes U.S. citizens among the freest people in the world. But how was our political system created, and what were the intentions of the people who created it? How fair and effective is our political system today? What changes, if any, does the system need?

This course will address these questions by examining the following issues:

1. What did the American Revolution mean for the different groups of people that were affected by it?
2. What impact does the American Revolution have on the United States today?
3. Why was the U.S. Constitution written and how does it work?
4. What role did the "Founding Fathers" such as Washington and Jefferson play in the founding of our country's political system and what did they contribute to our way of life?

Art History (Roy)

How do you feel about a work of art when you look at it? What do you like about it and what shapes those impressions? Art holds a language and history that is unique in itself, and we will attempt to better our understanding of it. In this class, we will be looking at what significance art has had in the past and is having in contemporary times. By looking at painting, drawing, photography, and sculpture, and seeing what effect they have had on each other and other mediums of art, we will work at broadening our understanding of what we can get from having art in our lives. Students will attend weekly exhibitions, and be responsible for short analyses of the exhibitions. A final oral presentation will also be required.

Autobiography Writing Workshop (Becky)

How do people tell the stories from their youth? What do they choose to tell and what do they leave out? In this course you will be reading excerpts from the autobiographies of different kinds of people. You'll be examining the way that people represent their childhood and adolescence. You'll also do your own autobiographical writing as you decide what your most important memories are.

This course is a writing workshop. There will be a focus on writing—your writing and other students' writing. Small groups of students/writers will work together on all of your pieces—brainstorming, discussing, revising, and editing them.

Brew Editorial Board (Student-Run)

Note: Students interested in being editors—in charge of layout, photography, illustration, or general planning—should sign up for the J period *Brew Editorial Board*. This will be a student-run committee.

Ceramics (Judy)

Introduction to making pottery and clay sculpture. We will study techniques and styles from all over the world, from past to present.

Students will learn visual and technical skills that will be used to help them develop their own styles. Finished work will be displayed in a schoolwide art exhibition.

(This class will be held in our JREC Pottery Studio here in the building.)

Chemistry of Household Products (Barry)

Are some types of soaps and toothpastes really better than others? In this course students will study what it is like to be a chemist by designing and carrying out experiments to test the claims made about different household products (e.g., soaps, toothpastes, cleansing creams, shampoos, etc.). Students will also make their own products and analyze what happens to them in chemical reactions. Each student will be required to record observations and data collected in laboratory notebooks. Lab reports will be required after each project is completed. Students will be expected to become familiar with the chemists' shorthand of writing formulas and reactions. Each student will be required to conduct an independent experiment at the end of the course that can be expanded to fulfill the requirements of a science proficiency. There will be an additional period each week when students can receive additional help with reading assignments.

Cults (Karen)

As the clock ticked closer to 12 midnight to ring in the new year and the beginning of the new millennium many people thought that something unusual was going to happen—something very scary, perhaps. As of yet, nothing has. But as many have pointed out, the new millennium has not yet really begun—so watch out!

Behind some of the apprehension was the fear that one of the many religious cults out there was getting ready to do something. But what is a cult? And why is there always an atmosphere of gloom and doom about them?

In this class we will take a closer look at a few of the groups that have been labeled as being cults by our society. We will look at who joins them, what they teach, and what they hope to accomplish.

Students will be expected to do an independent research project as well as completing various assignments. Your work will be evaluated based on this and your overall performance in and out of class.

Geometry A: Angles and Triangles (Terry W.)

This class will look at angles and shape relationships of all sorts from theoretical and practical viewpoints. You will look for patterns, systems, and structures in the material, do group proofs, and devise practical ways of measurement in class and out of class. We will also try some logic proofs.

Students will work mainly in small groups and there will be regular homework, puzzles, small group projects, and periodic quizzes.

Prerequisite: Teacher Recommendation

Geometry B: Angles and Triangles (Wally)

This class will look at angles and shape relationships of all sorts from theoretical and practical viewpoints. You will look for patterns, systems, and structures in the material, do group proofs, and devise practical ways of measurement in class and out of class. We will also try some logic proofs.

Students will work mainly in small groups and there will be regular homework, puzzles, small group projects, and periodic quizzes.

Prerequisite: Teacher Recommendation

Growing-Up Stories (Gail)

What makes a childhood memory important enough to write about? How do the important experiences of childhood influence adulthood? When an adult writes in a child's voice, are we convinced? Is something lost or gained?

The novels, stories, and excerpts we will be reading all tell of childhood experiences. Be ready to read, write, and discuss.

This is a good first literature course, but students with some experience studying literature are welcome.

Gym—E and J (Nancy and Terry W.)

In this class you have the opportunity to play sports, practice skills, exercise, jog, stretch. Either on your own or in cooperation with the others in the class, you will be able to take advantage of the gym.

Homer (Karen)

One of the most important figures in Greek literature was the writer Homer. His stories *The Iliad* and *The Odyssey* will be the centerpiece of our studies, but we will also take a look at some of the other myths written. In our analysis of these ancient myths we will attempt to understand what lessons, if any, these stories teach us, and try to determine if they are at all relevant today.

Students will be expected to keep up with the readings assigned and to participate in class discussions. Your work will also be evaluated based on the quality of the papers and projects that you will be asked to submit.

Horticulture, Advanced (Nancy)

In this class, you and everyone else will be doing individual experiments. Students usually come into this class to begin their science proficiency. This means that you should have a working knowledge of how to set up an experiment and carry it out. Those of you who have a proposal or who have done a pilot study will be able to get down to work immediately on your experiments. Those of you who need to play around with ideas will probably need another semester to complete your experiment.

Horticulture, Introduction (Nancy)

While learning about plants and their growth, you will learn how to do science: how to ask a testable question, collect relevant data, make conclusions, and be critical about what you have done. This class combines hands-on experiences with the necessary background reading and research. Since our evaluation is based upon how much you challenge yourself, you may take this class several times, but remember that you will be expected to work harder than the first time you took this course. You will be expected to arrive to class on time and have all relevant homework completed. During class time you will be expected to work independently and in cooperation with others. A final research paper is required.

Horticulture, Landscaping (Nancy)

In this class we will be planting plants, amending the soil, and tending to the beds that surround St. Catherine Park. You will learn how to design a bed, use tools, fertilize plants, mulch, and water plants outside. Working independently in a small group is paramount. Those of you who are working minimalists need not apply. *(Please note that this class will not count as a prerequisite for the science proficiency.)*

Just Bill (Phyllis)

Suppose Shakespeare wasn't "Shakespeare" but just Bill, an actor of the late 16th Century who wrote a collection of popular (though unpublished) plays, and was clever at making a comfortable living from showbiz. Would people still find his work extraordinary today? Would you?

We'll examine Bill's work from a number of perspectives to explore the best way to approach his plays. We'll read 'em, attend 'em, view 'em, perform 'em, and adapt 'em. We'll study the playwright and his times. Students will write a series of papers examining the Just Bill experience and evaluating his worth for the Century's patrons of the theater. We'll cover the tragedies (*King Lear*), the histories (*Richard III*), and comedies (*Comedy of Errors*, and *Taming of the Shrew*). Be prepared to spend some evenings at the theater to see how others have interpreted Bill.

Latin American Fiction (Phyllis)

As North Americans, we have been trained to look to Europe for our literary models while ignoring our own hemisphere and the great writers who have been steadily producing great books. In this class we will sample the rich literary tradition of Latin America and examine the ties between fiction and truth, magic and realism.

The reading list will include *Of Love and Other Demons* (Marquez—Colombia), *In the Time of the Butterflies* (Alvarez—Dominican Republic), *The House of the Spirits* (Allende—Chile), and *Dreaming in Cuban* (Garcia—Cuba).

Little Big Books (Alex)

This literature course focuses on short influential novels that demand interpretation. In class discussions we will work together to decipher the deeper meaning in these books. There will be five required essays, focusing on basic literary interpretation and comparative analysis.

This course will involve a lot of reading and writing. We will read approximately a book a week. In addition to the five papers, students will take quizzes, prepare class presentations, and write a final exam. *Note*: Two of the required papers in this course can be rewritten to satisfy the literature proficiency prerequisite. But taking this course does not ensure that the prerequisite paper requirement will be met.

Looking for an Argument (Avram and Herb)

This course will look at controversial issues and try to analyze them from conflicting viewpoints. The teachers will argue opposing positions and students will be encouraged to join in (and to select debate topics).

Students will take notes during each debate and every week will write an in-class essay on the topic being discussed that week. The in-class essays are aimed at giving students time-limited, pressured writing experiences that they can expect to encounter in any decent college. Students will need to use their notes in order to write these weekly essays.

No homework will be assigned in this class.

Math Lab (Becky and Rachel B.)

If you are taking algebra or geometry, and are not yet proficient in decimals, fractions, proportions, percents, and signed numbers, then this lab will be an add-on to your class. You'll play games, manipulate manipulatives, discuss puzzles and problems with each other, and count slices of a pizza pie. This class will help you pass the calculation prerequisite of the math proficiency.

Mechanics (Terry)

What's the best way to measure something? How can we find out how fast an object is moving? What measuring tools are the most accurate? This Physics course will address all of these questions. Students will conduct many hands-on experiments, and will be required to write lab reports. Most class work will be completed in small groups. Homework will be assigned regularly.

This class is only open to students who have passed Algebra 2.

Modern China Seminar (Avram)

Many historians argue that China in the 20th century has experienced as much dramatic change as any society on the face of the earth. This seminar will attempt an understanding of the ways in which China has changed in this period. It will begin with an examination of the philosophical traditions in Chinese thought and proceed to an exploration of China's interaction with Western nations in the 19th Century, an investigation of the events that culminated in the Communists coming to power in 1949, an evaluation of China's development under the leadership of Mao Tse Tung, and a consideration of China's attempt to mix elements of socialism and capitalism in the post-Mao era. We will analyze these topics by reading the work of historians who interpret from significantly different perspectives. We will also peruse a number of important primary sources. Most of the written work will involve writing a final paper on one of the major topics.

Novels (Barry and Gail)

Would you like to read more? Can't get started? Don't know what you like to read? Have never enjoyed reading novels? Have never read a novel? Do you enjoy talking about the books you do like?

This course is for you!

You will choose the books you read. You will decide if you enjoy them. You will discuss the ideas and issues that can be found in books. You will get recommendations and ideas from your classmates.

Occupying America: The Mexican-American and American Indian Political Movements (Marcela and Rachel B.)

In this course we will examine how young people during the 1960s and 1970s who were outside of mainstream, White America decided to make changes for themselves and for their communities. Through personal stories, primary and secondary historical documents, and short pieces of fiction we will explore how and why young people responded to these and other questions:

Should you do what your elders think is right, or make your own way, even if it means breaking ties with your traditions? Should you walk out of high school in order to force change in your education, or work hard to prove yourself within the system? Should you assert yourself as a woman within a political movement if you feel it is dominated by a male point of view, or stay quiet to present a united front? Should you demand the right to speak your own, non-English language in school? Should you occupy Alcatraz Island with the radical American Indian Movement (AIM) to demand change, or work with the Bureau of Indians (BIA) to improve life on the reservation? Should you show loyalty to the United States and fight in Vietnam, or protest the country's involvement?

We will compare and contrast the histories of young Mexican-Americans and American Indians—some of whom joined the political movements, and some of whom chose to work in other ways to make change.

Photo F (Rachel B.)

Are you interested in, or are you connected to, the people who work in your neighborhood deli, people at your community service, the kids who play ball on your block or hang out in your neighborhood? For this course you will choose a group of people—you may or may not be a part of it—that you are interested in documenting. The community may be an immigrant group, a family, friends in the neighborhood, or people who are drawn together because they love doing the same things.

What brings these people together? How is the community similar to or different from other groups of people who spend time together? How are the interests and needs of the individuals in the group supported by the larger community? What is the relationship that this community has to New York City?

Throughout this semester you will use your camera as a lens by which to capture what you think is most important and interesting about your chosen community. You will also be conducting interviews, writing your own observations, and collecting other objects and information that will help you put together your final project. In order to stimulate our creativity and critical eyes we will use many of our Friday afternoons to view the work of other photographers. An afternoon session is required on Tuesdays.

Playing God (Terry G.)

Scientists now have the ability to create, alter, and end life. Are these decisions that mere humans should be making? Are we using science to overstep the boundaries of what we should be doing? But if these procedures can reduce some suffering, can we refuse to study them?

We will address these questions and more in this scientific ethics course. Students will be required to read literature and original scientific papers. There will be regular written homework assigned as well as research papers. Students will be required to do several oral presentations before the class. This is not a hands-on science class.

Plays and Playwriting (Rachel W.)

A young woman struggles to recover from an incestuous relationship with her uncle. A boy slyly tortures his uptight teacher. A man with a sock fetish must hide the truth from his fiancée. A close friendship nearly dissolves when one of the girls learns she's pregnant.

At its best, theater is a place where stories, true and fantastical, come dramatically to life. The stories above are just a few of the dramatic stories previous years' plays classes saw presented both in the theaters of New York, where students usually attend more than six plays, and here at Urban, where students write their own short plays and then work with a playwright and several actors, who eventually performed the students' work.

This year, too, we will go to see plays (New York has the best theater in the country!), including plays chosen by the class together. We will read and discuss plays in class. Then we will work with professional actors and playwrights to write our own short plays. Students are required to attend several plays both during and after the school day.

Probability and Statistics (Wally)

This class will cover probability theory so that we can apply it to real-life problems (statistics): sample spaces, bias and fairness, confidence of answers, conditional probability, table analysis, standard deviation, regression analysis, all of the kinds of averages, prediction, and choice. We shall analyze newspaper studies on medicines, rare events as AIDS, and breast implants.

Solving puzzles and playing games are the basic procedures of the class and you will work mainly in small groups. Your job, as usual, is to figure things out and explain how you did the work.

Prerequisite: Teacher recommendation.

Project Adventure (Becky)

Love to climb? Scared of heights? A little bit of both? If you've ever wanted to walk a tightrope, balance ten people on a swinging log, sign your name on the ceiling of the gym, or climb a mountain, join Project Adventure. In this course, students will get the chance to challenge themselves and to see what a group of people can do when working together. There will be a focus on teamwork, creative problem-solving, and pushing yourself to do more than you think you can.

Public Speaking (Alex)

Do you get nervous when you have to speak in front of a group of people? Does your voice get lost in the crowd? Do you dread presentations? Do people keep telling you to "speak up"?

If you answered yes to any of these questions, take this class and conquer your fears! As a group, we will explore breathing, voice, enunciation, and memorization techniques. Each student will be responsible for memorizing, practicing, and presenting at least three "pieces." These can be speeches, monologues, poems, or stories. (Students who are interested in preparing acting monologues can use this course to help them prepare.) For a final presentation, each student must prepare a speech to be performed in front of the entire school.

Scene Study (Alex)

This acting workshop will focus on scene study. Students in the course will prepare a scene with a partner (or partners) to be performed for the class each Friday. This means each student will be responsible for reading plays, memorizing lines, rehearsing scenes, and preparing character research. All this work will be done outside of class. Students who sign up for this course must be prepared to work independently with their partners after school. If you cannot stay after school at least once a week, do not sign up for this class.

During the Friday afternoon classes, we will workshop the scenes students have prepared. This means scenes will be shaped and refocused, toward a goal of squeezing the maximum amount of drama from each scene.

In the second half of the semester, the class will collaborate on a production that showcases the scene work members have done. This will not be another "Cabaret"-style production, but rather a play, or collection of short pieces, that focuses on the acting process. The emphasis throughout the course will be on the craft of acting, not the final production.

Science Projects (Barry and Terri G.)

This course is open only to those students who must complete their data collection so that they can finish their science proficiency. These designated students *must* register for this class.

Slang Dictionary (Becky)

Yo yo yo! This will be the bomb!

What? Your favorite words aren't in *Webster's Dictionary*? Well, they'll be in ours. Come with suggestions of words to include.

Social Documentary Photography (Roy and Herb)

This course utilizes the lens of the camera and the photographer's eye to observe aspects of our society. Each student will choose an individual topic and, once it is approved, pursue it for a semester. A final product must be produced, which may be an exhibit, a book, or a class publication.

In addition to the student's individual projects, this class as a whole will be asked to complete a group project, possibly an Urban Academy calendar. Students will be expected to shoot, edit, and be responsible for completing the group project decided upon:

1. punctually complete in and out of class assignments
2. work together with other group members while handling various individual responsibilities well
3. attend a three to five Thursday darkroom session every week

Students wishing to take this class should have previous photographic experience or receive the consent of one of the instructors. Passing grades will be given only upon the completion of an acceptable class and individual publication. We welcome the participation of students who like to challenge themselves and want to know they've achieved something by the end of a course.

Spanish Reading and Conversation (Marcela)

Are you a Spanish speaker who sometimes feels uncomfortable speaking in Spanish? So you know how to read in Spanish but feel like you read very slowly? This class is intended to help build speaking and reading confidence, comprehension, and vocabulary through practicing the language. We will read Spanish magazine and newspaper articles, short stories, and essays. We will also be having discussions in Spanish about the readings and other topical issues.

Stretch and Go (Karen)

In this class we will focus on building tone and definition through stretching. A great deal of emphasis will be placed on tightening the stomach muscles, but we will certainly pay attention to other areas (arms, legs, etc.). Once we get through stretching, students should expect to "go" running, walking, or to do some other low-impact aerobic activity to complete the session. Students must remember to come prepared!

Supreme Law (Rachel W. and Harry)

Should a Rastafarian be allowed to keep his dreadlocks in the Navy? Should the police be allowed to search through your locker in school? Should Secret Santa be outlawed since it brings a quasireligious activity into a public school? What evidence should be allowed at your trial for murder? What do these questions have in common?

These are issues that the Supreme Court has ruled on, and they all affect your individual rights. In this class we will examine several constitutional questions by reading Supreme Court cases, by talking to lawyers and other legal experts, and by arguing about the cases in class. We will also pick a case the Supreme Court is slated to hear this spring, read related cases, and then travel to Washington, DC to watch the Supreme Court in action.

During the semester, you will be expected to act as a lawyer and judge on different cases examined by the class.

There will be an advanced seminar for a few interested students in this class who would like to meet additional times with Harry, investigate case law in greater depth, and, if appropriate, complete their Social Studies proficiency.

Textiles (Terri G.)

Crocheting, knitting, quilting, weaving—all of these techniques can be used to create and/or beautify cloth. Students in this independent study will work with a technique of their choice. Students must have some background in the technique that they choose.

The Figure (Marcela)

The human figure has been depicted in a wide variety of poses, mediums, and styles. It has been a key subject matter in art in many cultures and for many centuries. This course will focus on the figure in three ways:

1. We will work on figure drawing techniques by using live models (US).
2. We will experiment with rendering the figure using various mediums, styles, and contexts.
3. We will create a group mural project that incorporates figures as a main theme.

The Jazz Age (Karen)

It has been said that jazz music is "America's only true art form." Whether or not one agrees with this there is no question that jazz music and jazz musicians like Duke Ellington and others have certainly made a profound impression on American culture. This music, developed largely in the 1920s, helped to set the tone for and era that saw its fair share of drama. Gangsters, flappers, prohibition, and the stock market crash of 1929 were a few of the more notable highlights of this time.

We will study this period in America's history and listen to a fair share of the music of this era. Through the writings of F. Scott Fitzgerald and others, we will uncover what those who came of age during this time had to say about it.

As this class is interdisciplinary in scope, students will be reading both fiction and nonfiction. There will be a number of papers and several field trips. Class discussion will also play a role in your final evaluation.

Throwing (Nancy)

An analysis of skill in sports will show that the ability to throw is essential. Football and baseball are two sports where throwing is obvious; but if you look closely at racquet sports like tennis, squash, and racquetball, you will see that the throwing motion is involved especially in the service. Don't let your life slip away not knowing how to play a sport. Learn the basics. Open up your options and yourself to new experiences.

Trigonometry F (Terry W.)

This class will cover identities, proofs, triangles, equations, patterns, and graphing. You will plan solutions to practical problems and use a hands-on approach to problems outside of the classroom. You will work mainly in small groups, and will have regular homework, quizzes, and tests.

Prerequisite: Teacher Recommendation

Trigonometry I (Terry W.)

This class will cover identities, proofs, triangles, equations, patterns, and graphing. You will plan solutions to practical problems and use a hands-on approach to problems outside of the classroom. You will work mainly in small groups, and will have regular homework, quizzes, and tests.

Prerequisite: Teacher Recommendation

Trumpet—Playing God, The Sequel (Dorinda)

An experienced, professional trumpet instructor will take any and all interested in learning to play this instrument.

One mandatory, after-school, individual tutorial will be provided to assist you.

Try it—you'll like it!

Working in a Series (Marcela)

Working in a series allows artists to work in depth with concepts that they find particularly compelling. Working in a series also allows artists to develop their own style. This class will focus on creating a personal visual vocabulary that students can use in a variety of ways across many media. Initial assignments will concentrate on building skills and working in a series. Students will then have to develop a more complete body of work centered on a theme or themes of their choice. Sketchbook assignments are a crucial part of this course.

Yearbook (Rachel and Roy)

In this class we will produce the yearbook for Urban Academy. We will be documenting the life of the school on a weekly basis. We will try to develop creative, original ideas for the yearbook without losing the pizzazz of yearbooks from years past. We will try to put the yearbook out before the final crush at the end of the year, and we will be spending lots of time in the darkroom. Students who wish to take this class should be proficient in the darkroom and have some basic computer skills.

Yoga (Annalisa B.)

This class is for the stressed-out and out-of-shape who are looking to get into shape as well as the stressed-out well-muscled dancers, basketball players, weight-lifters, etc. who are looking to further strengthen and tone their bodies.

In the class we will combine traditional yoga postures, muscle conditioning, stretching, and controlled breathing to sculpt a leaner, stronger body while releasing stress and fatigue.

Yoga will meet only twice a week—Tuesdays and Thursdays—and will extend 10 minutes into the lunch period on Thursdays. The Friday class period will be a study period.

EXHIBIT 5
HODGSON VOCATIONAL–TECHNICAL HIGH SCHOOL
BEST PRACTICES

Academy of Manufacturing and Pre-Engineering

The Academy curriculum blends the study of computer-aided design, machining, electronics, material science, pneumatics/hydraulics, software applications, and statistical process control. Students are encouraged to participate in field trips, job shadowing, internship experience, and cooperative work experience.

Senior Project

An Exhibition of Achievement is a yearlong learning process incorporating student research and the preparation of a research paper, the development of a career-related product, and a final public exhibition of knowledge before a panel of experts from business and industry. Through the Senior Project, it is the school's goal to significantly improve student achievement and to help all students learn to use their minds well.

Effective with the class of 1998 school year, all students are required to successfully complete their Senior Project in order to earn a high school diploma.

Senior Project is the capstone event for all Hodgson students. Senior Project represents an authentic assessment of students' knowledge of their career area, as well as a measure of academic proficiency in research, writing, and communication skills. With the completion of Senior Projects, students will have successfully demonstrated their knowledge by integrating academic and vocational components of their school program and will be well prepared to compete at the postsecondary school level or in the world of work.

Core Academic Teams

Ninth-grade students are organized by core academic teams consisting of English, World Cultures, and Biology courses. Teachers plan these three subjects in an integrated way, often using a common theme. Core teams have the flexibility to regroup according to student learning styles and needs. A fourth period has been added to core team so students are afforded additional time for instructional enrichment, reading, project work, or to extend time in core courses. The remainder of the ninth-grade student's courses include Physical Education, Mathematics, and the Exploratory Program. A core team concept is also available at the 11th grade, merging American History and English courses.

Block Scheduling

Most of our courses are on a block schedule of 90 minute classes for a semester (90 days), versus the traditional 45-minute class. A block schedule results in more instructional time for the student, less subjects to concentrate on at a single time, and a new schedule after the second semester. There are several variations in the Hodgson block schedule to accommodate instructional priorities.

Extra Help Program: Saturday Academy, Tuesday and Thursday Tutoring

Saturday Academy is a 2-hour enrichment, tutoring, and makeup session extended to students each week from 9:00–11:00 a.m. using faculty tutors. Also, students are afforded tutoring and makeup sessions on Tuesday (2:30–3:30 p.m.) and Thursday (3:00–5:30 p.m.). On Tuesday, there is a 4:00 p.m. activity bus for transportation to take students as near to their homes as possible.

No Credit (NC) Status Attendance Policy

Students who reach six (6) school day absences in a semester will be placed on No Credit status until their attendance obligations have been met. Students can earn course credit and remove NC status by attending extra help sessions on Tuesday, Thursday, Saturday, and/or by attending special extra-help sessions on a prearranged basis with their teacher(s). NC status must be resolved no later than 2 weeks after the end of the marking period, or NC status becomes an F grade.

Last year, Hodgson students achieved a 95.1% daily attendance rate. This is the highest rate ever attained, and meets the District's standard of excellence.

Employability Rating System

Each marking period, students are rated by their career instructors on key employability indicators. By rating student performance through employability indicators, we anticipate improving student skills necessary for successful employment. Students who might not otherwise be identified as good workers by academic standards can be identified, rewarded, and motivated through the employability rating system. This system is a useful tool for employers in their hiring practices along with school grades and attendance records.

References

Ancess, J. (1994). *Inquiry high school: Learner-centered accountability at the Urban Academy.* New York: National Center for Restructuring Education, Schools, and Teaching, Teachers College, Columbia University.

Ancess, J. (2000, June). The reciprocal influence of teacher learning, teaching practice, school restructuring, and student learning outcomes. *Teachers College Record, 102* (3), 590–619.

Ancess, J., & Darling-Hammond, L. (1994). *The senior project: Authentic assessment at Hodgson Vocational/Technical High School.* New York: National Center for Restructuring Education, Schools, and Teaching, Teachers College, Columbia University.

Ancess, J., & Ort, S. (1999). *How the Coalition Campus Schools have re-imagined high school: Seven years later.* New York: National Center for Restructuring Education, Schools, and Teaching, Teachers College, Columbia University.

Ancess, J., & Ort, S. (2001, January 13). *Making School Completion Integral to School Purpose & Design.* Paper presented at conference on Dropouts in America: How Severe is the Problem? What Do We Know about Intervention and Prevention? Harvard Graduate School of Education, Cambridge, MA.

Anderson, C. S. (1982). The search for school climate: A review of the research. *Review of Educational Research, 52,* 368–420.

Apple, M. (1990). *Ideology and curriculum.* New York: Routledge.

Baker, R., & Gump, P. (1964). *Big school, small school: High school size and student behavior.* Stanford, CA: Stanford University Press.

Baker, W. (1983). Floor trading and crowd dynamics. In P. Adler & P. Adler (Eds.), *Social dynamics of financial markets* (pp. 107–128). Greenwich, CT: JAI.

Bidwell, C. E. (1965). The school as a formal organization. In J. G. March (Ed.), *Handbook of organization* (pp. 972–1019). Chicago: Rand McNally.

Boyer, E. (1983). *High school.* New York: Harper & Row.

Bridges, W. (1991). *Managing transitions: Making the most of change.* Cambridge, MA: Perseus Books.

Bryk, A. (1994, Fall). More good news that school organization matters. *Issues in Restructuring Schools, 7,* 6–8.

Bryk, A., & Driscoll, M. E. (1988). *The high school as community: Contextual influences and consequences for students and teachers.* Madison, WI: National Center on Effective Secondary Schools.

Chambers, J. G. (1981). An analysis of school size under a voucher system. *Educational Evaluation and Policy Analysis, 3,* 29–40.

Coleman, J. S. (1988). Social capital in the creation of human capital. *AJS,95,* Supplement S95–S120.

Conant, J. B. (1959). *The American high school today: A first report to interested citizens.* New York: McGraw-Hill.

Corwin, R. D. (1965). *A sociology of education.* New York: Meredith Publishing

Darling-Hammond, L. (1997). *The right to learn: A blueprint for creating schools that work.* San Francisco: Jossey-Bass.

Darling-Hammond, L., & Ancess, J. (1996). Democracy and access to education. In R. Soder, (Ed.), *Democracy, education and the schools* (pp. 151–181). San Francisco: Jossey-Bass.

Darling-Hammond, L., Ancess, J., & Falk, B. (1995). *Authentic assessment in action: Studies of schools and students at work.* New York: Teachers College Press.

Darling-Hammond, L. Ancess, J., McGregor, K., & Zuckerman, D. (2000). Inching toward reform in New York City. In E. Clinchy (Ed.), *Creating new schools: How small schools are changing American education.* New York: Teachers College Press.

Darling-Hammond, L., Ancess, J., & Ort-Wichterle, S. (2002, Fall). Reinventing high school: An analysis of the coalition campus schools project. *American Education Research Journal, 39* (3), 639–673.

Darling-Hammond, L., & Snyder, J. (1992). Framing accountability: Creating learner-centered schools. In A. Lieberman (Ed.), *The changing contexts of teaching* (pp. 11–36). Chicago: NSSE.

Darling-Hammond, L., & Snyder, J. (1993). *Creating learner-centered accountability.* New York: National Center for Restructuring Education, Schools, and Teaching, Teachers College, Columbia University.

Dewey, J. (1966). *Democracy and education.* New York: Macmillan. (Original work published 1916)

Eccles, J. S., Midgley, C., Wigfield, A., Buchanan, C. M., Reuman, D., Flanagan, C., & MacIver, D. (1993). Development during adolescence: The impact of stage-environment fit on young adolescents' experiences in schools and families. *American Psychologist, 48,* 90–101.

Elmore, R. (2000). *Building a new structure for school leadership.* Washington, DC: Albert Shanker Institute.

Etzioni, A. (1993). *The spirit of community: Rights, responsibilites, and the communitarian agenda.* New York: Crown Publishers.

Fine, M. (1989). Silencing and nurturing voice in an improbable context: Urban adolescents in public school. In Giroux, H., & McLaren, P. (Eds.), *Critical pedagogy, the state and cultural struggle* (pp. 153–173). Albany, NY: State University of New York Press.

Fine, M. (1991). *Framing dropouts.* Albany, NY: State University of New York Press.

Fine, M. (1998). What's so good about small schools? In M. Fine & J. I. Somerville (Eds.), *Big schools, big imaginations: A creative look at urban public schools.* Chicago: Cross City Campaign for Urban School Reform.

Fuller, B., Wood, K., Rapoport, T., & Dornbush, S. M. (1982). The organizational context of individual efficacy. *Review of Educational Research, 52,* 7–30.

Gladden, R. (1998). The small schools movement: A review of the literature. In M. Fine & J. I. Somerville (Eds.), *Small schools, big imaginations: A creative look at urban public schools.* Chicago: Cross City Campaign for Urban School Reform.

Glasser, W. (1992, May 13). Quality, trust, and redefining education. *Education Week* (pp. 25, 32).

Goodlad, J. I. (1984). *A place called school: Prospects for the future.* New York: McGraw-Hill.

Goodlad. J. I. (1996). Democracy, education, and community. In R. Soder (Ed.), *Democracy, education and the schools* (pp. 87–124). San Francisco: Jossey-Bass.

Grant, S. G. (2001, June). An uncertain lever: Exploring the influence of state-level testing in New York State on teaching social studies. *Teachers College Record, 103* (3), 398–426.

Greene, M. (1995). *Releasing the imagination: Essays on education, the arts, and social change.* San Francisco: Jossey-Bass.

Hodgson Vocational–Technical High School. (1990). *Mission Statement.* Newark, DE: Author.

Hodgson Vocational–Technical High School. (1998). *Mission Statement.* Newark, DE: Author.

Howley, C., & Bickel, R. (2002). Reducing effects of poverty on achievement: 4-state study [On-line]. *American School Board Journal.* Available: http://www.asbj.com /2000/04/0400beforetheboard.html [2002, 6-03-02].

Institute for Education in Transformation, The. (1992). *Voices from the inside: A report on schooling from inside the classroom.* Claremont, CA: Claremont Graduate School.

International High School. (1985). *The International HS Mission Statement.* Long Island City, NY: Author.

International High School. (1993). *Project PROPEL handbook.* Long Island City, NY: Author

Kerr, D. H. (1996). Democracy, nurturance, and community. In R. Soder (ed.), *Democracy, education and the schools* (pp. 37–68). San Francisco: Jossey-Bass.

Lee, V. E., Bryk, A. S., & Smith, J. (1993). The organization of effective secondary schools. *Review of Research in Education, 19,* (pp. 171–268). Washington, DC: AERA.

Lee, V. E., & Loeb, S. (2000, Spring). School size in Chicago elementary schools: Effects on teachers' attitudes and students' achievement. *American Education Research Journal, 37* (1), 3–32.

Lee, V. E. & Smith, J. (1994, Fall) High school restructuring and student achievement: A new study finds strong links. *Issues in Restructuring Schools, 7,* 1–5.

Lee V. E. & Smith, J. (1996, February). Collective responsibility for learning and its effects on gains in achievement for early secondary school students. *American Journal of Education, 104,* 103–147.

Lee, V. E., Smith, J., & Croninger, R. G. (1995, Fall). Another look at high school restructuring: More evidence that it improves student achievement, and more insight into why. *Issues in Restructuring Schools, 7,* 1–10.

Levesque, K., Lauen, D., Teitelbaum, A., Alt M., & Librera, S. (2000). Vocational Education in the United States: Toward the Year 2000 [on-line]. Available: http://nces.ed.gov/pubs2000/qrtlyspring/9cross/q9-1.html#H4.

Louis, K. S., Kruse, S. D., & Marks, H. M. (1996). Schoolwide professional community. In F. Newmann & Associates (Ed.), *Authentic achievement: Restructuring schools for intellectual quality.* San Francisco: Jossey-Bass.

McLaughlin, M. W. (1994, Fall). Somebody knows my name. *Issues in Restructuring Schools, 7,* 9–11.

McNeil, L. (1986). Contradictions of control: School structure and school knowledge. New York: Routledge & Kegan Paul.

Meier, D. (1995). *The power of their ideas: Lessons for America from a small school in Harlem.* Boston: Beacon Press.

Merriam, S. B. (1988). *Case study in education: A qualitative approach.* San Francisco: Jossey-Bass.

Mitchell, G. D. (1968). *A dictionary of sociology.* Chicago: Aldine Publishing.

Nadelstern, N., & Boso, A. (2001). *The International High School 2000–2001 annual report.* Long Island City, NY: International High School.

National Center for Education Statistics. (1995a). *High school and beyond longitudinal study of 1980 sophomores (HS&B-So: 1980/1992) high school transcript study.* Washington, DC: U.S. Department of Education.

National Center for Education Statistics. (1995b). *National Assessment of Educational Progress (NAEP) 1990 and 1994 high school transcript studies.* Washington, DC: U.S. Department of Education.

New Castle County Vocational Technical School District. (1994). *District performance report.* Newark, DE: Author

New Castle County Vocational Technical School District. (2001, August). *Performance indicators: Report card for the school year 2000–2001.* Newark, DE: Author

Newmann, F. M. (1981). Reducing student alienation in high schools: Implications of theory. *Harvard Educational Review, 51,* 546–564.

Newmann, F. M. (1993, Fall). Director's overview. *Issues in Restructuring Schools, 5,* 2.

Newmann, F. M., & Associates. (1996). *Authentic achievement: Restructuring schools for intellectual quality.* San Francisco: Jossey-Bass.

Noddings, N. (1992). *The challenge to care in schools: An alternative approach to education.* New York: Teachers College Press.

New York City Board of Education. (2001). *School Report Cards* [On-line]. Available: http://www.nycenet.edu/

Oakes, J. (1985). *Keeping track: How schools structure inequality.* New Haven, CT: Yale University Press.

Oakes, J. (1995). Great news–greater challenges. *Issues in Restructuring Schools, 7,* 11–13.

Paul M. Hodgson Vocational High School. (1990). *Hodgson Mission Statement.* Newark, DE: Hodgson.

Paul M. Hodgson Vocational High School. (1998). *Hodgson Mission Statement.* Newark, DE: Hodgson.

Powell, A. G. (1996). *Lessons from privilege: The American prep school tradition.* Cambridge, MA: Harvard University Press.

Powell, A. G., Farrar, E., and Cohen, D. K. (1985). *The shopping mall high school.* Boston: Houghton Mifflin.

Proulx, A. (1993). *The shipping news.* New York: Simon & Schuster.

Raywid, M. A. (1988, Winter). Community and schools: A prolegonenon. *Teachers*

College Record, 90 (2), 197–210.

Raywid, M. A. (1999). Current Literature on Small Schools. (ERIC Document Reproduction Service No. ED 425049 99). Available: http://www.ed.gov/databases/ERIC_Digests/ed425049. html

Rist, R. C. (1973). *The urban school: A factory for failure.* Cambridge, MA: MIT Press.

Rosenbaum, J. (1976). *Making inequality: The hidden curriculum of high school tracking.* New York: John Wiley & Sons.

Rowan, B. (1990). Commitment and control: Alternative strategies for the organizational design of schools. *Review of the Research in Education, 16,* 353–389.

Rugger, K. (1991). Literature activities for the first half. In Motion Team (Ed.), *Motion* (pp. 13–38). Long Island City, NY: International High School.

Sedlak, M., Wheeler, C., Pullin, D., and Cusick, P. (1986). *Selling students short.* New York: Teachers College Press.

Senge, P. (1990). *The fifth discipline: The art and practice of the learning organization.* New York: Doubleday.

Sizer, T. R. (1984). *Horace's compromise.* Boston: Houghton Mifflin.

Sorensen, A. B., & Hallinan, M. T. (1986). Effects of ability grouping on growth in academic achievement. *American Education Research Journal, 23,* 519–542.

Steinmetz, S. (1997). *Random House Webster's college dictionary.* New York: Random House.

Urban Academy. (1994a). *Points of view, Spring 1994.* New York: Author.

Urban Academy. (1994b). *Urban Academy requirements for graduation.* New York: Author.

Urban Academy. (2001). *Urban Academy course catalog, Spring 2001.* New York: Author.

Urban Academy Laboratory High School. (1993). *Why?* New York: Author. (Original work published 1991)

Waller, W. (1932). *The sociology of teaching.* New York: Russell & Russell.

Washburn, S. L. (1960). Tools and human evolution. *Scientific American, 203*(3), 63–75.

Wasley, P., Fine, M., Gladden, M., Holland, N. E., King, S. P., Mosak, E., & Powell, L. (2000). *Small schools, great strides: A study of new small schools in Chicago.* New York: Bank Street College of Education.

Wehlage, G. G. (1993). Social capital and the rebuilding of communities. *Issues in Restructuring Schools, 5,* 3–5.

Wehlage, G., Rutter, R. A., Smith, G. A., Lesko, N., & Fernandez, R. R. (1989). *Reducing the risk: Schools as communities of support.* Philadelphia: Falmer Press.

Wilson, F. R. (1998). *The hand: How its use shapes the brain, language, and human culture.* New York: Pantheon Books.

Index

About the Author

Jacqueline Ancess is co-director of the National Center for Restructuring Education, Schools, & Teaching (NCREST) at Teachers College, Columbia University. Her research and publications have focused on urban school reform, small schools, and school restructuring, assessment, and accountability. For more than 20 years Ancess worked in the New York City school system, where she taught English in the South Bronx, was the founding director of Manhattan East (a small school in District 4), and was the Director of Educational Options in Districts 2 and 3, where she led big-school restructuring and small-schools development. She was awarded with the New York Alliance for the Arts Schools & Culture Award for her work at Manhattan East. She is co-author of *Authentic Assessment in Action: Studies of Schools and Students at Work* (1995, Teachers College Press).